Ken Spours and Ann Hodgson recently won second prize in the Society for Education Studies 2010 book awards for their co-authored title *Education for All: The future of education and training for 14-19 year olds* (with Richard Pring, Geoffrey Hayward, Jill Johnson, Ewart Keep, Alis Oancea, Gareth Rees and Stephanie Wilde, Routledge, 2009).

Here is some praise for their new book, ***Post-Compulsory Education and Lifelong Learning across the United Kingdom:***

'This is another authoritative analysis of post-compulsory education and training, from an expert research team with an excellent reputation. The authors exploit in-depth the opportunity to contrast differences between the four UK countries, and draw important lessons from these comparisons. This volume provides very solid and valuable policy analysis to help lifelong learning make progress in the next decade.'

Tom Schuller, Director of the Inquiry into the Future of Lifelong Learning and Director of Longview, Co-author of *Learning Through Life*

'Neoliberal globalisation and the current recession are forcing governments around the world to reconsider the way post-compulsory education is funded, organized and governed. In many cases, market-oriented reforms and budget cuts are in tension with cherished principles such as accessibility, equality of opportunity and educational quality. This insightful and timely collection carefully examines these dynamics with special attention to the role of national states, local governments, the market and civil society in policy-making and program delivery. In their comparative analyses, the authors show how similarities in funding priorities, policy decisions and program delivery coexist with differences that derive from the history, culture and political arrangements of each country. This book illuminates our understanding of cross-national convergence and divergence patterns in policy formulation.'

Daniel Schugurensky, School of Public Affairs and School of Social Transformation, Arizona State University, USA

'This book explores the complex and contested field of post-compulsory education and training across the systems of the UK. It bravely navigates the inter-related areas of curriculum, qualifications, provider arrangements and learning cultures in the context of parliamentary devolution and the growth of distinctive policy agendas in the constituent countries. The influential policy analysts and thinkers who have contributed to this book present us with a really useful and up-to-date analysis of policy networks, political narratives and governance as they affect the future of post-16 education and training in the UK.'

John Polesel, Professor of Education, Graduate School of Education, The University of Melbourne, Australia

'A fascinating, timely and stimulating contribution to the field of post-compulsory education and lifelong learning. It's excellent to see the tradition of "home international" comparisons in the UK being continued and developed within this important text. The chapter on the new Coalition Government is a must read for all researchers.'

Dr Roy Canni   **:otland**

'This book, by leading writers in the field, makes a major contribution to analyses of policies concerned with post-compulsory education and lifelong learning in the UK. The book usefully draws the readers' attention to the continuities, ruptures and contradictions in the education policies developed by the home nations. One of the key strengths of the book is its commitment to policy learning as opposed to policy borrowing, with another being its refusal to portray the education policy of any one of the home nations as inherently superior.'

James Avis, Professor of PCET, University of Huddersfield

Post-Compulsory Education and Lifelong Learning across the United Kingdom

The Bedford Way Papers Series

A full list of Bedford Way Papers, including earlier books in the series,
can be requested by emailing ioepublications@ioe.ac.uk

Post-Compulsory Education and Lifelong Learning across the United Kingdom

Policy, organisation and governance

Edited by Ann Hodgson, Ken Spours and Martyn Waring

Institute of Education, University of London
Bedford Way Papers

**Leading education
and social research**
Institute of Education
University of London

First published in 2011 by the Institute of Education,
University of London, 20 Bedford Way, London WC1H 0AL

www.ioe.ac.uk/publications

© Institute of Education, University of London 2011

British Library Cataloguing in Publication Data:
A catalogue record for this publication is available from the
British Library

ISBN 978 0 85473 904 2

Typeset by Quadrant Infotech (India) Pvt Ltd
Printed by Elanders

Contents

Notes on contributors

Professor Jim Gallacher is Emeritus Professor of Lifelong Learning at the Centre for Research in Lifelong Learning, Glasgow Caledonian University.

Dr Stuart Gardner is Head of Business Performance at the Young People's Learning Agency.

Professor Vernon Gayle is Professor of Sociology in the Department of Applied Social Science at the University of Stirling.

Dr Dennis Gunning is the former Director of Skills, Higher Education and Lifelong Learning in the Welsh Assembly Government's Department for Children, Education, Lifelong Learning and Skills. He retired in July 2010.

Professor Ann Hodgson is Faculty Director of Research, Consultancy and Knowledge Transfer and Co-Director of the Centre for Post-14 Research and Innovation at the Institute of Education, University of London.

Professor David James is Co-Director of the Bristol Centre for Research in Lifelong Learning and Education (BRILLE) at the University of the West of England, Bristol.

Professor Ewart Keep is Deputy Director of the Economic and Social Research Council's Research Centre on Skills, Knowledge and Organisational Performance (SKOPE) at Cardiff University.

Dr Janet Lowe CBE FRSE is a member of the Scottish Funding Council, a board member of Skills Development Scotland and Chair of their joint Skills Committee.

Professor David Raffe is Professor of Sociology of Education at Edinburgh University and a member of the University's Centre for Educational Sociology.

Professor Gareth Rees is Director of the Wales Institute of Social and Economic Research, Methods and Data and a Professor in the School of Social Sciences at Cardiff University.

Professor Ken Spours is Head of the Department of Continuing and Professional Education and Co-Director of the Centre for Post-14 Research and Innovation at the Institute of Education, University of London.

Martyn Waring is a Visiting Research Associate at the Institute of Education, University of London.

Contributors whose responsibilities involve, or have involved, work on behalf of government agencies are writing in a personal capacity.

Foreword

David Raffe

This book analyses the organisation and governance of post-compulsory education and lifelong learning in the United Kingdom, and especially in England, Scotland and Wales. It discusses how these have changed since the 1990s, over a period when new ideas of public management, democracy and accountability have called into question governance arrangements within each home country and when devolution has changed the relationships between them.

At the heart of the book are the changes associated with, or consequent on, the establishment of the Scottish Parliament and the National Assembly for Wales in 1999. Political devolution held out three promises. First, it promised to end the democratic deficit. Each country would be able to choose policies to reflect its own values, aspirations and circumstances; to the extent that these led in different directions, policies would diverge. Devolution would apply the principle of subsidiarity, which unionist governments had always demanded for the UK within Europe, to the home countries within the UK. Second, devolution promised – or was seen to promise – a more open, participative and inclusive model of democracy. It would redistribute power within each country as well as between the UK and devolved levels of government. Third, devolution would lead to the creation of a 'UK policy laboratory', in which all countries would learn from rigorous and dispassionate comparisons of their different policies. Except for the third, these promises applied primarily to Scotland and Wales (and, in a very different context, to Northern Ireland). Issues of democracy and governance have also been salient in England, but their connection to devolution is more tenuous, although it has exposed the absence of an 'English' level of government. Indeed, the failure of English policy-makers to recognise that devolution has implications for England, with the problems that result, is a sub-theme of this book.

Have these three promises been fulfilled? The chapters of this book provide a wealth of evidence and argumentation on all three. With respect to the first promise, to end the democratic deficit, several chapters comment on policy differences across the home countries. A more neo-liberal emphasis in England, with a focus on the supply of skills, is contrasted with a stronger social-democratic orientation and greater emphasis on skill demand and utilisation in Scotland and Wales. However, we may question the extent to which these differences reflect different national values, aspirations and circumstances: public attitudes and values tend to be rather similar across the three countries, and policy differences are at least partly the result of different political systems. We may also question the extent to which policy differences are the product of political devolution. Many of these differences preceded political devolution; national path-dependence is another theme of these chapters, which present more evidence of difference than of divergence. Moreover, much of the divergence that has occurred can be attributed, not to new directions by the devolved administrations, but to changes in English policy. The book illustrates the complexities of policy-making across the UK and shows (for example) how the interdependence of the different systems, together with their shared dependence on UK-wide institutions such as the labour market, put severe constraints on divergence. Although policies have, on balance, tended to diverge since 1999, this is not a predetermined trend. The chapters on Scotland and on Wales both suggest that the current recession may result in renewed convergence in important areas of policy.

Devolution has, however, led to divergence in the 'education state' – the institutions and structures of governance – of each home country. These education states are increasingly distinctive and non-parallel, resulting in different agendas, processes and logics of policy-making in each country. To what extent do they also fulfil the second promise of devolution, to introduce a new model of democracy? Once again, the chapters provide substantial evidence of relevant policy differences. They contrast the top-down, centralised patterns of control in England with more inclusive and collaborative arrangements, and greater proximity between policy-makers and providers, in Scotland and Wales. At the same time, the book also notes that these differences cannot all be represented as divergence or as the products of political devolution. The smaller size of Scotland and Wales, their greater institutional homogeneity and their different political and professional traditions all facilitate a more consensual, inclusive style of policy-making – and did so before 1999.

However, we should be wary of idealising the Scottish or Welsh position. 'Providers' as a group may play a stronger role in policy-making in those countries, but that does not mean that every teacher or lecturer feels included. As we have observed in Scotland, a collaborative, consensual mode of governance can easily lead to an unreflecting, conservative, producer-driven policy style in which hierarchies are unchallenged and consensus is mistaken for evidence. The current challenge to find new modes of governance is just as pressing in Scotland and Wales as in England, and the book suggests that this may be a new area of convergence.

One of the disappointments of devolution is the substantial failure, documented in many of these chapters, to make a reality of the 'UK policy laboratory'. (At least, if this laboratory exists, its staff lack training in scientific method.) Part of the reason is institutional; in contrast to most federal or quasi-federal systems, the current UK structures make little systematic provision for inter-government relations and provide no forum for this systematic learning. Part of the reason is cultural, however, a legacy of former asymmetrical relationships and of the politics of identity. When analysts and policy-makers *have* tried to learn from other home countries, they have often done it badly: they have confused policy learning with policy borrowing and the search for 'good practice' (a tendency which the term 'policy laboratory', with its connotations of experimentation, may encourage). Especially in England, policy analysts who have tried to learn from the other home countries have often viewed them uncritically: the grass always seems to be greener on the other side of the border.

However, the book provides at least three indications, if not of a fully-equipped laboratory, at least of growing interest in the potential for policy learning from 'home international' comparisons within the UK. The first is the work of the UK Commission for Employment and Skills, which has been an important channel of communication, and of exchange of evidence and experiences, across the UK. The second, more speculative, is the suggestion that the home countries will need to learn from each other as they explore new modes of governance to suit straitened circumstances. The third is the publication of this book itself, and the growing interest among the research and policy communities of which it is a reflection. By offering a more detailed, nuanced and triangulated account, and representing the perspectives of different home countries and of policy-makers as well as researchers, the book takes us beyond simplistic comparisons, policy borrowing and idealisations. We can learn from each other's failures as well as successes, from their problems as well as solutions, and from the parts of their systems that resist change, as well as from the areas of innovation. After all, if the grass is always greener on the other side of the border, this could be because it never stops raining.

Preface

It is common for governments in individual countries to look beyond their national boundaries when developing policies for the future. In doing so, they may be influenced by the apparent success of a new approach in tackling a common problem. It could be that a particular country has come to be regarded as a world leader, perhaps on the basis of international comparisons of performance. Sometimes an incoming administration with a very different agenda to its predecessor will look to learn from governments of a similar political persuasion that have been in power for a period elsewhere and, therefore, had the opportunity to implement policies similar to those it now intends to pursue.

The field of education and training is no exception to this quest to learn from international comparators. Effective investment in education and skills is typically seen as one of the most important barometers for maintaining and improving a country's international competitiveness. Here in the UK, successive governments have looked to draw on evidence from a wide range of countries – EU member states, the USA, old Commonwealth countries such as Australia and Canada, successful economies in south-east Asia and, more recently, Nordic countries – to help inform the development of new initiatives and programmes.

Yet the UK does not itself have a unified and homogeneous education and training system. There are long-standing differences between the four nations that comprise the UK, albeit with some important unifying features. As a direct result of parliamentary devolution since 1999, the differences between these systems have grown as each country's national government (or the UK government in the case of England) pursues policy directions it considers best suited to its own particular traditions, needs and circumstances.

Notwithstanding the willingness to draw lessons from other countries, there is little evidence of any desire on the part of policy-makers in the separate countries of the UK to learn from each other's experiences. Indeed, it could be suggested that in many respects the reverse is true. Each country, particularly in the case of the three smaller ones, wants to see itself as having a separate national identity, and this reinforces the tendency towards adopting overtly distinctive policies and programmes. Does this mean that the individual nations are missing opportunities to learn from experiences that, arguably, could be regarded as highly pertinent to their own circumstances? Conversely, does increasing divergence mean that we are creating the scope for much greater 'policy learning' between the constituent parts of the UK in the years to come? If so, what are the prospects that we will avail ourselves of these opportunities?

These are the types of question that underlie the themes in this volume. The book arises out of an Economic and Social Research Council (ESRC) Teaching and Learning Research Programme sponsored seminar series, entitled 'New directions in learning and skills in England, Scotland and Wales: Recent policy and future possibilities', which took place during 2008–9. Rather than attempting to cover all aspects of education and training, the seminar series focused primarily on post-compulsory education and lifelong learning, excluding higher education. It was inspired by evidence of accelerating change in policy and governance arrangements in this area, allied to a sense of increasing divergence between different parts of the UK fuelled by parliamentary devolution. We wanted to understand what lay behind these changes and what impact they could be expected to have.

One of the strengths of the seminar series, which we have replicated in this book, is that it brought together policy-makers, researchers and practitioners from England, Scotland and Wales, all with a keen interest and wealth of experience in the issues under discussion. Our contributors are all recognised authorities in their fields, able to draw on the latest thinking and policy developments to inform their analyses.

Throughout the volume we have incorporated messages and themes that arose during the earlier seminar discussions, as well as material from papers and presentations prepared exclusively for the seminars and wider-ranging literatures on policy-making and governance in education and training. These have further enhanced the richness and diversity of input to what is undoubtedly a complex, controversial and highly topical debate that has potential resonance well beyond the field of post-compulsory education and lifelong learning. The issues raised in the book about convergence and divergence of policy between the constituent parts of the UK can be seen as directly relevant to a much wider debate about the future of the UK state as a political entity.

Events in education and training, which is a high-profile policy area, can move on very quickly. This means that publications inevitably become dated in some respects, particularly as regards the detail of particular programmes or governance arrangements. The writing of this book, spanning the May 2010 UK general election, means that the risk is perhaps higher than normal. We have tried to ensure that the details included in the book are correct and up-to-date at the time the text was finalised for publication (at the beginning of September 2010). We have also sought to incorporate as much relevant material as possible about the changes being introduced by the new UK Conservative–Liberal Democrat Coalition Government. However, this is intended more as a forward-looking book than an historical analysis. With that in mind, particularly in the final two chapters, we have attempted to address possible future scenarios very much in the context of the new UK Government's political make-up and approach. Although the details of particular policies, programmes and governance arrangements will change, for the foreseeable future the underlying analytical themes in this book will, we believe, remain highly relevant to debates in this relatively under-researched area.

The book will be of direct interest and relevance to national and international researchers and policy-makers in the broadly defined field of post-compulsory education and lifelong learning. We hope it will also appeal to members of teacher and lecturer professional associations and unions, officials from national and regional agencies and organisations in England, Scotland and Wales, and students on postgraduate courses related to education and political science.

Acknowledgements

As is clear from the contents and preface, many people have contributed, directly or indirectly, to the compilation of this volume.

The editors would first want to thank the Economic and Social Research Council (ESRC) for their sponsorship, through the Teaching and Learning Research Programme, of the seminar series without which this book would not have been conceived. The ESRC funding also helped to facilitate an initial meeting of potential contributors to the book. We see the book as one important means of ensuring that findings from the research are disseminated to a wider audience and that this helps to inform future policy development in ways that can promote the interests of learners, in line with the underlying aims of this ESRC programme.

We also offer enormous thanks to our main contributors, who have warmed to their tasks and engaged positively with the themes of the book as a whole. In many cases, people have gone beyond providing their individual chapters or sections, by contributing constructive and helpful comments and suggestions on other parts of the book, in particular the important opening and final chapters. This has, undoubtedly, helped produce a more coherent and integrated final text and, we believe, significantly improved the accuracy and rigour of the volume as a whole. We are very grateful to all our contributors for their efforts in helping us keep to the deadlines for publication, particularly when we know this has sometimes coincided with demanding pressures at work or from personal circumstances.

Several people have made invaluable contributions to particular chapters and sections of the book. We have sought to acknowledge these at the appropriate points in the text. They fully deserve special mention in this section as well. Our appreciation goes to Frank Coffield, Bryn Davies, Carmel Gallagher, Ruth Leitch, Linda McTavish, Sally Power, Charlie Sproule, Judy Stradling, Chris Taylor and Richard Wyn Jones.

Finally, it would be a gross omission not to mention the contribution of those, too numerous to mention individually, who participated in one or more of the five seminars that provided so much of the stimulus for this book. We were continually impressed and enthused by the quality of debate at these events. Had it been otherwise, the book would almost certainly never have been contemplated. We hope that all these people will get to read it. If so, we hope that it will enable them to recall some of the discussions and, perhaps, to identify a thought or line of argument that they helped to prompt in the first instance.

Chapter 1

National education systems: The wider context

Ann Hodgson and Ken Spours

Rationale and aims of the book

Much writing on education focuses on schools. This book explores what is happening beyond schooling and discusses what is often referred to in the international literature as 'lifelong learning' (e.g. Tuijnman and Schuller, 1999). The importance of extending initial education and training for young people, as well as ensuring that adults have access to learning across the life course, has become increasingly recognised by national governments as they grapple with the challenges of globalisation, technological change and, more recently, a widespread recession. The way that lifelong learning is funded, organised and governed is a hotly debated topic internationally since these matters can have a profound influence on wider political objectives, such as increasing access to opportunities, greater equity and improving quality of life.

As the title suggests, this book looks at how post-compulsory education – education and training beyond the age of 16 but excluding higher education – is organised within the United Kingdom (UK), with a particular focus on England, Scotland and Wales. In several important respects, the UK continues to exist as a single economic and political entity. There is a UK government with a recognised UK economy, and major policy areas such as defence, economic and foreign policy are decided at the UK level. Viewed internationally, the different peoples and countries of the UK – England, Scotland, Wales and Northern Ireland – can be seen to share important system, social and cultural features.

However, there are underlying national and regional differences, and these are becoming more evident. They are to some extent historical. England has always been the dominant entity, with a population more than five times that of the other three countries combined. Scotland, though much smaller, has fostered its own national identity for centuries. Wales, on the other hand, at least in governance terms, has been much more closely integrated with England, although, over the past two decades, it too has developed a distinctive sense of national purpose (Morgan, 2002). Back in the 1980s, both countries were sufficiently different to England to resist much of the neo-liberal reform associated with Thatcherism and retained many of the features of the previous Keynesian era. These underlying differences were given further scope to influence developments following parliamentary devolution in 1999, when Scotland and Wales achieved their own elected parliament and assembly, respectively, with important though still limited powers. Northern Ireland is, however, a different case. Its population continues to be divided in its political and cultural orientation. One community (predominantly Protestant) still looks to the UK (or more precisely England) for its identity, while the other (predominantly Catholic) sees a future within a united Irish entity.

These commonalities and differences across the UK continue to be played out in wider politics and inform many areas of policy, including education and training. It was against this background that five seminars, funded by the Economic and Social Research Council (ESRC)[1] deliberated the organisation and direction of development of post-compulsory education and lifelong learning in England, Scotland and Wales. The seminar series, which took place between 2008 and 2009, did not discuss issues from Northern Ireland directly, although this book includes some reference to relevant developments there.

The seminar series provided the stimulus for this volume. However, its authors go well beyond the discussions that took place and also reflect on the changes that have occurred during the first few months after the election of a new UK Conservative–Liberal Democrat Coalition Government in May 2010. Contributions to the book chart changes in the organisation and governance of post-compulsory education and lifelong learning in England, Scotland and Wales since 1997, with a particular focus on the period from 2007 onwards.

Throughout the text we use the term 'governance' alongside the narrower term 'government'. By 'governance' we mean the broad political and organisational arrangements at national, regional and local levels, including the roles of policy formation, policy mechanisms and those involved in the policy-making process. While this term is contested and interpreted in different ways in the literature (e.g. Hajer and Wagenaar, 2003; Kooiman, 2003; Newman, 2005), we find it useful because it connotes a wider set of relationships than the term 'government', crossing public and private boundaries as well as embracing both the state and civil society (Ball, 2008). The term 'governance' allows for an exploration of the different levels and configurations of power in complex political and organisational formations. It also prompts a focus on how policy is interpreted, translated, mediated and enacted at different levels of the system and how this impacts on sites of learning and the professionals and learners within them.

At the outset, due to the historical and policy differences described earlier, seminar participants grappled with a range of terminology to describe the same area of education. In England, for example, 'post-compulsory education and lifelong learning', which was used in policy discourse from 1998 to 2001, has more recently been referred to as 'learning and skills' or even the 'further education (FE) system'. In Scotland and Wales, however, the term 'lifelong learning' has continued in use. Later in the chapter, the reasons behind the different uses of terminology are investigated further. Throughout the book we will use the term 'post-compulsory education and lifelong learning' to describe all publicly-funded provision from 16+ outside higher education institutions. However, in the cases of England and Wales we will also include discussion of the education of 14–19 year olds since this has been a major policy focus in the two countries and, to a lesser extent, in Northern Ireland, and is seen as an important aspect of initial post-compulsory education. We do not comment in detail on higher education, because this is a huge area in its own right and would make the scope of the book too broad. Nevertheless, we do refer to the effects of the higher education system on post-compulsory education and lifelong learning, in particular the relationship between further and higher education via Foundation Degrees and Higher National Diplomas, because of the way in which it impacts on the provision of lifelong learning, most notably in Scotland.

During the seminar series, the various aspects of post-compulsory education and lifelong learning, and particularly policy developments, were always viewed within their wider economic, political, social and cultural contexts. This helped participants understand prevailing trends as well as the potential for, and limitations on, further change. Of specific interest were the ways in which the 'education state' (Hodgson and Spours, 2006) has been developing within the three countries, the different modes of governance and versions of democracy, and the role of national agencies and their relationship with education providers. As the seminar series developed, there was an increasing focus on how different approaches to policy and organisational developments affected learners and their learning.

The seminar series concluded by considering future trajectories and scenarios for post-compulsory education and lifelong learning in England, Scotland and Wales. Participants discussed whether processes of national divergence in governance, a strong trend over the past decade, would continue and if so, in what form and with what effects. Could it be that the post-compulsory education and lifelong learning systems in each of the three countries would look radically different in ten years' time, with each of them locked into a particular 'path of dependency'? At the same time, other wider socio-economic developments, including the global economic crisis, suggested there could be pressures towards further convergence in some respects. Was it possible that amidst the contrasts in education policy and governance, fundamental economic problems might reassert a UK paradigm? Differences and commonalities could be viewed in yet another way. Could the variations between countries, for example in terms of socio-economic deprivation and affluence and between rural and urban localities, outweigh those between countries, so that educational experience is not so much determined by in which country you live, but where you live within that country? This discussion raises questions about the roles of the various levels of governance – national, regional, local and institutional – in determining education policy and outcomes.

An issue that recurred throughout the series, but entered the debate strongly in the final seminar, was whether the closer you got to the learner and the learning experience, the less difference there appeared to be between the three countries, especially if compared internationally. Was it the case that national differences that seemed so apparent at the 'meso' structural and governance levels were not strongly reproduced at the 'macro' UK and the 'micro' learner levels? The seminars explored an apparent paradox. On the one hand, classrooms look rather similar in England, Wales and Scotland, full-time learners study similar subjects and programmes in schools and colleges, the curriculum is overwhelmingly conducted in English, and apprenticeships follow similar patterns in all three countries. On the other hand, and when looked at through the lenses of access, equity and quality, differences began to appear. Policy and funding priorities affect which learners are able to access publicly-funded education and training, what financial contribution they have to make and the quality of the environment in which they study. These tensions of commonality and difference are explored throughout the book.

The seminar series and the book bring together perspectives from researchers, policy-makers and practitioners involved in post-compulsory education and lifelong learning systems in England, Wales and Scotland. The seminars facilitated a process of shared knowledge production and mutual learning. The series as a whole produced a rich, up-to-date and highly textured source of evidence in an under-researched area. Economists, political and social scientists and education specialists debated issues with policy-makers from national and local government in all three countries and with practitioners from a range of post-compulsory education and lifelong learning providers. All participants were committed to developing new understandings of a complex and fast-changing picture to inform future research, policy-making and practice in an area which was recognised as being fundamental to the economic and social well-being of the three nations involved.

Key features of the systems in England, Scotland, Wales and Northern Ireland

It is useful to look at commonalities and differences between the four countries of the UK through the lens of wider international comparison.

Continental European initial post-secondary education and training systems can be categorised in a number of ways (see for example Green *et al.*, 1999; CEDEFOP, 2009).

First, there is a distinction to be made between those systems that are more education-based (e.g. the UK where most young people remain in full-time education in schools and colleges until the age of 18 or 19) and those where a significant proportion of young people will be undertaking learning in the workplace through apprenticeships (e.g. Germany or Switzerland). Second, there are education and training systems which are highly centralised (e.g. France where the curriculum and schools are under the direct control of national ministries) and those which are more devolved with increasing levels of responsibility handed to local authorities, schools and colleges (e.g. Finland and Sweden). Education and training systems can also be distinguished according to how far state functions have been privatised and the extent to which a market in institutional relations is encouraged to operate. In this respect, the UK system, more particularly England, can be viewed as highly market-driven compared with other European systems, and located much nearer to other Anglo-Saxon systems, such as the US and New Zealand. By way of contrast, education and training can be conceived and operated under social partnership agreements between the state, trade unions and employers. This is a feature, for example, of Nordic and Germanic systems.

Viewed through these different perspectives, the UK systems as a whole can be seen as predominantly education-based, with a relatively minor role for the workplace and social partnership. That is to say, the 'macro-feature' of the weak relationship between the education and training system and the labour market makes them quite distinct from the Nordic and Germanic models. On the other hand, each of the four countries of the UK differs in terms of the level of devolution and centralisation and the degree to which the market dominates the language of governance and the behaviour of its schools, colleges and work-based providers. Here, as we will see in later chapters, England stands out as having taken privatisation and a market-driven approach much further than Scotland and Wales since the mid-1980s (see also Ball, 2007). In terms of devolution of power, Scotland and Wales have retained a more powerful role for local authorities in the governance of schools and community education, while England, under both Conservative and New Labour administrations, became more centralised, operating through a large number of 'arm's length', non-ministerial agencies (e.g. the Further Education Funding Council and the Learning and Skills Council), which appropriated many of the powers that had resided at the local level (Coffield *et al.*, 2008).

Subsequent chapters will detail the different governance and organisational arrangements in England, Scotland and Wales. Here we briefly summarise the key system features in each of the countries in order to provide the reader with a 'map' to navigate a way through later chapters (see Table 1.1).

Table 1.1 Key features of the four UK country systems: April 2010

	England	Scotland	Wales	Northern Ireland
Political control and approach	New Labour Government from 1997 pursuing managerialist, neo-liberal policies. Skills seen as essential to improving economic competitiveness and helping to promote social inclusion.	Skills policy initially similar to England under Labour–Liberal coalition. The Scottish National Party (SNP) has adopted a distinctive approach since 2007: emphasis on a lifelong skills strategy with greater focus on skills utilisation.	Consistent political direction under Labour–Liberal and Labour–Plaid Cymru coalitions, with greater emphasis on social democratic principles such as social partnership and inclusion. Particular concerns over skills utilisation given decline of long-standing industries.	Power-sharing government from 2006 between Unionist and Republican communities. Emphasis in skills policy on economic competitiveness and overcoming the sectarian divide.
Departmental responsibility	Two separate departments [Dept. for Children, Schools and Families (known as Department for Education since May 2010) and Dept. for Business, Innovation and Skills] with divide at age 19.	Since 2007 unified structure for post-compulsory education and lifelong learning with a single Cabinet Secretary responsible for both.	Single department [Dept. for Children, Education, Lifelong Learning and Skills (DCELLS)] responsible for all aspects of education and training.	Two separate departments [Dept. of Education and Dept. for Employment and Learning (DEL)] with FE and HE coming under the stewardship of DEL.
Terminology	Learning and skills	Lifelong learning	Lifelong learning	Education and skills
Participation	To become compulsory to age 18 from 2015 through raising of the participation age.	To remain voluntary from 16.	To remain voluntary from 16, with policies to encourage participation.	To remain voluntary from 16.
Central/ local control	Predominantly top-down approach. Policy decisions heavily centralised and implemented through complex network of agencies. New 14–19 funding and commissioning responsibilities for local authorities from 2010.	Significant partner involvement in policy determination. Relatively strong professional and inspectorate influence. Funding for schools channelled through local authorities. Single funding council for FE and HE.	All former agencies (except HE funding body) absorbed into the Welsh Assembly Government (WAG). DCELLS has responsibility for policy development, delivery and implementation, and engages directly with providers. Strong role for local authorities.	Former support agencies were to merge into a new highly centralised Education and Skills Authority (ESA). Due to Unionist opposition the plan has not progressed and local Education and Library Boards remain in place.

	England	Scotland	Wales	Northern Ireland
Provider network and degree of competition	System encourages competition between a range of different types of institution. 14–19 collaboration encouraged, but problematic.	Network of largely uniform schools and FE colleges with distinct roles (focusing primarily on education and training respectively) and little competition. Policy emphasis on cross-sector collaboration and participation of voluntary sector.	Clear distinction between schools and colleges, although recent policy recognises need for collaboration in order to meet learner needs 14–19.	Clear distinction between schools and colleges, with the latter now regionalised into six 'super colleges'. Recent policy focus on collaboration 14–19.
Qualifications	Frequent reforms over past 30 years, particularly to applied and vocational qualifications. Regulation through Ofqual: private awarding bodies and Sector Skills Councils develop qualifications. Strongly tracked system – general, broad vocational, apprenticeship.	Distinct qualification system subject to frequent but relatively incremental reforms. Single awarding body (Scottish Qualifications Authority) for most school and majority of college qualifications. Unifying influence of comprehensive Scottish Credit and Qualifications Framework (SCQF).	Traditionally uses English-style qualifications. Recent development of distinctive Welsh Baccalaureate: a 'portfolio' award providing an overarching framework for all qualifications. Single Credit and Qualifications Framework for Wales (CQFW) in place.	The Council for the Curriculum, Examinations and Assessment regulates, sets and awards English-style general qualifications (i.e. GCSEs and A Levels) but not Diplomas. It also sets and awards vocational qualifications that are independently regulated by Ofqual.

In *England*, education policy is determined by two ministries – the Department for Education, which has responsibility for education and training up to the age of 19, and the Department for Business, Innovation and Skills, which oversees all forms of publicly-funded education and training beyond the age of 19. This age-related ministerial bifurcation has also affected the language of policy in England, with a loss of the term 'lifelong learning' as an overarching narrative. In England, the New Labour Government legislated to raise the age of participation to 18 by 2015 (the Coalition Government has not yet indicated its final view on this), whereas in Wales, Scotland and Northern Ireland compulsory education ends at the age of 16. Governance of the system is highly complex and has also been subject to frequent changes of approach in recent years, which has added to the sense of complexity (Coffield *et al.*, 2008). In the latter part of the New Labour Administration (1997–2010), democratically elected local authorities were given overall strategic responsibility for the commissioning of education and training up to the age of 19, but in conjunction with a range of arm's-length funding (e.g. the Young People's Learning Agency) and regulatory bodies (e.g. Ofsted and Ofqual). Funding for the education and training of 19+ learners is under the Skills Funding Agency. Schools, colleges and work-based training providers have high degrees of autonomy and compete for learners, although 14–19 policy under the New Labour Government also emphasised the need for collaboration between providers (DfES, 2005). At the same time, government policy over the last two decades has encouraged the establishment of different types of providers (e.g. academies, trust schools and 'free schools') to join a wide array of specialist schools, colleges and independent learning providers.

Qualifications are regulated by Ofqual, which reports directly to Parliament, but they are developed and marketed by a range of private awarding bodies. Currently young people have a choice of four major routes from the age of 16: General Certificate of Education Advanced Levels (A Levels) in a wide range of subjects; 14 lines of 14–19 Diplomas at Foundation, Higher and Advanced Level; Apprenticeships; and Foundation Learning programmes at Entry and Level 1. Entry to these programmes is selective and depends on the learner's prior attainment in General Certificate of Secondary Education (GCSE) programmes, which may take a more academic or a more applied form. Many 14–16 year olds now take a mixture of GCSEs and vocational programmes (including 14–19 Diplomas), although this will vary according to the provision available in their locality (Lynch *et al.*, 2010).

Scotland has a unified structure for post-compulsory education and lifelong learning, with a single Cabinet Secretary responsible for both. Schools and community education providers are funded via 32 local authorities. Post-school education and training and higher education were funded directly by two dedicated funding councils from 1999–2005, but in 2005 the two bodies were merged to form the Scottish Further and Higher Education Funding Council. As in England, colleges are self-governing institutions, having been given incorporated status since 1993. Institutional arrangements in Scotland are much simpler than in England, with the majority of young people studying in comprehensive schools up to the age of 17 and a minority moving into further education colleges for vocational programmes from the age of 16. Colleges in Scotland cater for a wide age range. Scotland has its own qualifications system and most school and college qualifications are developed and administered by a single awarding body, the Scottish Qualifications Authority (SQA). A comprehensive credit and qualifications framework – which claims to be the most developed in Europe – aims to include all qualifications in Scotland.

Wales has a single ministry – the Department for Children, Education, Lifelong Learning and Skills (DCELLS) – responsible for all aspects of education and training, although there is still some distinction in provision at the age of 19 because pre-19 learners have greater statutory entitlement than those who are aged 19 and above. A major change took place in 2006, when all the arm's-length agencies with responsibilities in the education and training field, except the HE funding council, were absorbed into the Welsh Assembly

Government (WAG). This means that the WAG's responsibilities now run right through from policy development to delivery and implementation, including decisions on funding allocations to post-16 providers. Local authorities have an established and distinctive role in relation to the funding and planning of school provision up to the age of 19. As in England, schools and colleges compete for 16–19 year olds, but there has been a much stronger drive towards collaboration (WAG, 2004 and 2006). While further education colleges are also incorporated institutions, the education provider market is less active in Wales, where there is some division of labour between schools, which primarily offer general education up to the age of 16 and in sixth forms, and colleges, which focus mainly on vocational courses and now also cater for the majority of post-16 students. Moreover, the push for institutional diversity so prevalent in England has not been pursued in Wales. Wales uses the same qualifications as England, but pursues its own regulatory agenda and has recently developed a distinctive overarching qualification in the Welsh Baccalaureate (see Chapter 4 for more detail on this award).

In *Northern Ireland* the Department of Education of Northern Ireland is responsible for the central administration of all aspects of school-based education and related services, except the higher and further education sector, responsibility for which is within the remit of the Department for Employment and Learning. The creation of separate ministries was partly a result of the need to provide sufficient ministerial portfolios to facilitate division of responsibilities across the range of political parties partaking in power-sharing. It had been planned that in January 2010 the five Education and Library Boards, the equivalent of local authorities in other parts of the UK, the Council for the Curriculum, Examinations and Assessment and the Regional Training Unit would merge into a new Education and Skills Authority. The intention was to bring both the policy and operational aspects of education and training within the remit of national government with an emphasis on raising standards, meeting targets and delivering efficiency gains (ESAIT, 2007). The formation of a large centralised agency reporting directly to the Department of Education has stalled due to political opposition from Unionist politicians. Meanwhile, further education colleges within Northern Ireland have been merged into six large regional organisations. The school system in Northern Ireland is still divided into 'maintained' (mainly Catholic) and 'controlled' (mainly Protestant) schools and, while the 11+ examination that determines secondary school entry has been officially abolished, both Catholic and state grammar schools are still effectively selecting pupils through their own admissions tests. In terms of qualifications, Northern Ireland still offers English-style awards – GCSEs and A Levels, as well as a range of vocational qualifications. Northern Ireland has not introduced the 14–19 Diplomas, but does intend to implement an Entitlement Framework in September 2013. From that date, schools will be required to provide pupils with access to a minimum number of courses at Key Stage 4 (current target 24) and at post-16 (current target 27). In both cases at least one-third of the courses must be general (academic) and at least one-third applied (vocational/professional/technical).

Similarities and differences

Education and training policy in England and Northern Ireland is overseen by two ministries, one largely responsible for schools and the other for post-school and adult education and training. In Wales and Scotland, on the other hand, responsibilities have been united under one ministry to reflect their stronger focus on 'cradle to grave' lifelong learning. The role of local authorities is more pronounced in Scotland and Wales, although the English system has been moving back in this direction more recently. Arm's-length agencies perform financial and regulatory functions in England, Northern Ireland and Scotland, with some formal separation between policy formulation and operation. Wales stands out in terms of its deliberate attempt to remove arm's-length agencies, and its more unified curriculum and qualifications system, although it shares this latter feature with Scotland. Northern Ireland's distinctiveness lies in its historical community divisions, which the Northern Ireland Assembly is attempting to address through a process of centralisation and mergers in terms of the governance of education and training. Scotland has the longest tradition of a distinctive education system separate from the English model and has developed its own particular national curriculum and qualifications approach, although its governance structures remain surprisingly similar to those in England. As later chapters in the book will indicate, the difference for Scotland lies more in the way that policy is formulated via professional dialogue, a feature that it shares to some degree with Wales. England remains distinctive because of its size, the complexity of its governance arrangements, its institutional diversity and the extent to which policy promotes an education market. In addition, England stands alone in passing legislation to raise the age of participation to 18, and this is likely to have an impact on the distribution of resources towards younger learners and away from adults. While Scotland, Wales and Northern Ireland all aspire to increased levels of participation in post-secondary education, their stance is one of encouragement rather than compulsion.

This structural overview of the ways in which the four countries of the UK organise their education and training system tells only a part of the story. There is another, less obvious narrative about how the systems work in practice, who is involved in the formation and implementation of policy and how these dynamics affect opportunities for learners. Later chapters will consider issues such as who participates, where people study, who pays, who becomes qualified and how far issues such as equity, quality and access pervade policy and practice. The analysis will seek to explore the extent to which these more complex and subtle aspects of the respective systems point to greater or lesser divergence than the structural descriptions outlined above might suggest.

Finally, the broader political landscapes of all the countries of the UK will receive serious consideration in subsequent contributions. There had been a crisis of political legitimacy in Scotland and Wales in the 1980s and early 1990s, arising from the existence of a Conservative Government in Westminster, when Labour and Nationalist parties attracted the vast majority of electoral support in these two countries (Trench, 2009). Both had developed distinctive characteristics in terms of governance and policy, although these tended to be more evident in Scotland than in Wales. The way that devolution was introduced in 1999 resulted in different powers for Scotland and Wales. Scotland acquired both legislative and executive powers, whereas initially Wales was granted only the latter. Recently Wales has started to gain more legislative powers, though in a rather patchwork and uncoordinated manner. Education and training, however, is one of the areas that has been fully devolved and thus has the potential for greater divergence. According to Trench, behind all this were pressures from both countries for greater levels of independence from Westminster and a Labour Government in England prepared to bow to these demands. However, as Chapters 7 and 8 point out, this fine political balance could well be disrupted by the election of a UK Conservative–Liberal Democrat Coalition Government.

Chapters in the book

This volume is divided into three major sections. Part 1 considers national contexts and approaches to policy. This is followed by a section on organisation, governance and practice. Part 3 concludes the book with two chapters devoted to possible future directions.

Chapter 2 seeks to explain the distinctive policy trajectory that England has followed over the last two decades or more on post-compulsory education and lifelong learning, by reference to its underlying ideological and theoretical bases and the associated concepts and images that have been generated as a result. It also probes some of the forces that are now starting to contest and disrupt this narrative, including the development by the devolved administrations of different and competing stories about where policy needs to go next. In particular, it considers the impact of the UK Commission for Employment and Skills as an institution that appears increasingly to be questioning the fundamental tenets upon which English skills policy has been founded.

Chapter 3 explores the distinctive approaches to policy development in post-compulsory education and lifelong learning in Scotland. While the chapter focuses mainly on developments post-devolution and the establishment of the Scottish Parliament in 1999, these are set in the context of earlier developments which continue to influence policy and provision. Two distinct phases of policy are identified – the first associated with the Labour–Liberal Democrat coalitions, which governed Scotland during the first eight years after devolution, and the second since the Scottish National Party (SNP) assumed control of the Scottish Government, following the elections in 2007. The chapter assesses the implications of these two approaches for the development of national structures, which have been established to enable the pursuit of different policy objectives.

Chapter 4 sets out to use the Welsh experience over recent times (and especially since the establishment of the National Assembly for Wales in 1999) to highlight three analytical themes relating to the development of post-compulsory education and lifelong learning. The first considers how far policy trajectories in Wales are 'path dependent', that is whether polices are shaped by what has gone before. The second theme focuses on the extent to which policies are underpinned by political ideology and the shaping role of powerful groups within Welsh civil society. The final theme is that of the wider political economy within which policies on post-compulsory education and lifelong learning are located. Again, the Welsh case is especially illuminating with respect not only to the constraints imposed on policy outcomes by the exigencies of wider economic conditions, but also to the equally significant effects generated by the funding imperatives embodied in the devolution settlement itself.

Chapter 5 provides a description of how the three national systems in England, Scotland and Wales are organised and operate in practice. The chapter reflects on patterns of learner participation and the issues these raise in their respective countries, current organisational arrangements and key debates, the future direction of policy and areas for further reform. In doing so, it raises issues about the nature and role of the state, the main policy players, and the relationship between national, regional and local governance and institutional arrangements in each of the countries. The chapter highlights implications for the conduct of policy and the effects of organisational arrangements on learners, education professionals and wider stakeholders, such as employers.

Chapter 6 presents an account of the consequences of policy processes and structures for providers, at the level of the further education colleges. The fundamental question here is whether (and, if so, to what extent) the sorts of differences that are discussed elsewhere in the book have an impact on practices. The chapter draws on interviews with senior college leaders from England, Scotland and Wales, including those who participated in the seminar series. It also makes use of the concept of 'learning culture' developed in an earlier Teaching and Learning Research Programme research project. Some key points of similarity and difference are signalled in the relationship between colleges and policy processes in England, Scotland and Wales. These concern contexts for collaboration, mission, voice and connectedness to policy and relationships to quality regimes.

Chapter 7 explores the role of the wider contexts of the state, markets and democracy in shaping the reform of public services and post-compulsory education and lifelong learning across the four countries of the UK. In doing so, it explores the processes of 'convergence' and 'divergence', as the relationship between the assemblies and parliaments of Scotland, Wales and Northern Ireland and the UK Westminster Government may be becoming more unpredictable. The chapter also touches on the concept of 'policy learning', why this has been so problematic across the four countries of the UK and what conditions might make it more possible. It concludes with a brief discussion of 'post-devolution politics' and what this might signify for the UK as a political entity.

Finally, *Chapter 8* draws together some of the key themes arising from previous chapters in the book and their influences on convergence and divergence between England, Scotland, Wales and Northern Ireland. The chapter then briefly discusses the new UK Conservative–Liberal Democrat Coalition Government's approach to policy in this area and suggests how this might affect the governments in Wales, Scotland and Northern Ireland. The book concludes with possible scenarios for the future of education and training policy in the UK and speculates about the extent to which policies in the four countries may diverge further in the future.

Note

1   We would like to acknowledge the funding of the seminar series by the ESRC – reference number 139-46-0003.

References

Ball, S.J. (2007) *Education Plc: Private sector participation in public sector education*. London: Routledge.

-- (2008) 'New philanthropy, new networks and new governance in education'. *Political Studies*, 56(4), 747–65.

Coffield, F., Edward, S., Finlay, I., Hodgson, A., Spours, K. and Steer, R. (2008) *Improving Learning, Skills and Inclusion: The impact of policy on post-compulsory education*. London: Routledge.

Department for Education and Skills (DfES) (2005) *14–19 Education and Skills*. London: DfES.

Education and Skills Authority Implementation Team (ESAIT) Northern Ireland (2007) *RPA Will Improve Education*. <http://www.esani.org.uk/rpa_will_improve_education.asp> (accessed 9 September 2010).

European Centre for the Development of Vocational Training (CEDEFOP) (2009) *Modernising Vocational Education and Training: Synthesis report on vocational education and training research in Europe*. Luxembourg: Publications Office of the European Union.

Green, A., Wolf, A. and Leney, T. (1999) *Convergence and Divergence in European Education and Training Systems*. London: Institute of Education, University of London.

Hajer, M. and Wagenaar, H. (eds) (2003) *Deliberative Policy Analysis: Understanding Governance in the Network Society*. Cambridge: Cambridge University Press.

Hodgson, A. and Spours, K. (2006) 'An analytical framework for policy engagement: The contested case of 14–19 reform in England'. *Journal of Education Policy*, 21(6), 679–96.

Kooiman, J. (2003) *Governing as Governance*. London: Sage.

Lynch, S., McCrone, T., Wade, P., Featherstone, G., Evans, K., Golden, S. and Haynes, G. (2010) *National Evaluation of Diplomas: The first year of delivery*. Department for Children, Schools and Families (DCSF) Research Report RR 220. London: DCSF.

Morgan, R. (2002) *Annual Lecture to the National Centre for Public Policy*. University of Wales, Cardiff.

Newman, J. (ed.) (2005) *Remaking Governance: Peoples, politics and the public sphere*. Bristol: Policy Press.

Trench, A. (2009) 'Devolution in Great Britain and the governance of learning and skills'. Presentation for 'New Directions in Learning and Skills in England, Scotland and Wales' seminar, Institute of Education, University of London, 18 February. <http://www.tlrp.org/themes/documents/hodgsonsem2/DevolutioninGBandtheGovernanceofLearningandSkillsAlanTrench.pdf> (accessed 12 March 2010).

Tuijnman, A. and Schuller, T. (eds) (1999) *Lifelong Learning Policy and Research: Proceedings of an international symposium*. London: Portland Press.

Welsh Assembly Government (WAG) (2004) *Learning Pathways 14–19 Guidance*. Cardiff: WAG.

-- (2006) *Learning Pathways 14–19 Action Plan*. Cardiff: WAG.

PART 1

NATIONAL CONTEXTS AND APPROACHES TO POLICY

Chapter 2

The English skills policy narrative

Ewart Keep

Introducing the limits of the possible

In England over the last quarter of a century or more, under both Conservative and New Labour administrations, a story or explanatory narrative around the issue of learning and skills policy was gradually constructed, refined and reinforced. This narrative expounded a 'gospel of vocationalism' (Grubb, 2004; Grubb and Lazerson, 2004) framed within a neo-liberal system of beliefs that suggested that as most other forms of state intervention in the economy and labour market are either impossible or undesirable, education and training and the supply of skills offers one of the few legitimate ways in which government can boost the fortunes of individual workers and of firms, as well as the economy more generally. The narrative's functions have been threefold:

1. To define the range of policy goals – social and economic – that education and training policy is to tackle, to explain how education and training could address these, and thereby to make the case for why political attention and resources should be devoted to education and training.
2. To establish the ideological beliefs, and resultant limits and boundaries, within which education and training policy (in terms of policies, programmes and institutions) can be debated and fashioned, thereby closing off consideration of alternative analyses and setting the direction of travel for policy development.
3. To encode a set of basic assumptions about how the education and training system can best be structured and managed by central government.

In essence, points 1 and 2 form the major element of the narrative, and point 3 the subordinate element. The narrative has always applied most strongly to further education (FE), vocational areas, adult learning and workforce development and training, and has had less hold over schools policy and higher education (HE), although in the case of the latter, HE increasingly came to be seen under New Labour as an adjunct to workforce development policies (see DIUS, 2008; BIS, 2009).

Those wishing to study policy documents that encapsulate the development and shape of the narrative should consult, for example, DfEE, 1998; Blunkett, 2001; LSC, 2001; DfES et al., 2003; DfES, 2004; DfES et al., 2005; LSC, 2005; Leitch, 2005 and 2006; and DIUS, 2007; alongside speeches given by previous Prime Ministers Blair (2007) and Brown (2007a and b). As this list suggests, the creation of the narrative has not been the work of a single government department – it has encompassed elements contributed or embellished by all the above-listed government departments, as well as by individual politicians, their advisors, senior civil servants and quango managers, and a variety of policy entrepreneurs (gurus, advisors and think-tank staff).

This chapter outlines the key components of the narrative and how it has been used to freeze English policy development within a particular conceptual framework that allows only a very constrained menu of policy moves. It then examines whether the narrative is likely to persist, evolve or collapse, given the changed fiscal circumstances and new government under which it now finds itself operating. Within the space available it is not possible to explore every facet of the narrative, nor to map out a comprehensive explanation for its development. Those seeking greater detail should consult Keep, 2009; Perry et al., 2010; and Keep et al., 2008.

The major elements of the narrative

The narrative has centred around a number of key elements or beliefs that establish a framework for analysing economic trends and for positioning education and training policy within them. These beliefs are not necessarily well evidenced, nor do they always mesh coherently with one another. In an important sense, as will be explored in more detail below, what they reflect is an appreciation of what ideology has told the policy-maker cannot be contemplated or attempted by way of analysis or intervention. The narrative in many ways thus represents what is left in terms of analytical space and available policy moves.

The first belief has been that globalisation is an unstoppable force and has created worldwide product, capital and labour markets, wherein the UK and its individual citizens/workers must compete (Blair, 2007; Brown, 2007a and b). The primary means of adjusting to these challenges has been seen as embracing the free market and in investing in the human capital of the workforce. More and better skills have thus come to represent, 'the most important lever within our control to create wealth and to reduce social deprivation' (Leitch, 2006: 2), with human capital now, 'the key determinant of corporate and country success' (Blair, 2007: 2). As a result, within a generally *laissez-faire* approach to economic policy, skills became one of the few areas where government could or should still seek to intervene, though not in terms of prescribing what employers ought to contribute. In many instances, the need for government interventions has been justified via the supposition that market failure must be acting to produce sub-optimal levels of outcome (see Keep, 2006a and b).

Given globalisation and heightened international competition, critical importance has been assigned to using international benchmarking of stocks of skills (as proxied by qualifications held by the national population or workforce – see Keep, 2008) as the starting point for policy formation. Benchmarking of skill stocks has provided the basis for the creation of a sense of national crisis (see Leitch, 2005 and 2006; and DIUS, 2007 for details), thereby enabling those fostering the panic to secure additional resources for education and training interventions. Such benchmarking has tended to concentrate on the outputs from other national education and training systems, rather than also on embracing their structure and systems of governance.

There has also been a firm belief that de-regulated, flexible labour markets deliver the best economic results (Blair, 2007; Brown, 2007a). Training should, therefore, be organised on a largely voluntary basis, with minimal prescription and regulation of what employers should be expected to provide. This belief has had major implications for who has been expected to fund the desired 'skills revolution' – namely that the state and individuals have had to dig deeper into their pockets. Employers have been exhorted to follow suit, but compulsion has usually been deemed impossible.

Insofar as the interests of workers need protecting, higher levels of skill have been viewed as providing them with the best safeguards against exploitation or poor quality work (Blair, 2007). This has been coupled with an underlying philosophy of how the labour market and the employment relationship function, founded on the notion that capital and labour ultimately have a single set of shared common interests, rather than an acceptance that the needs of employees and management may sometimes differ and that this will sometimes lead to conflict. As a result, the policy narrative has assumed that fundamental material differences between workers and managers do not need to exist, that conflict is the result of misinformation, and that, 'the best business works today as a partnership' (Blair, 2007: 6).

In terms of the changing structure of the labour market, the dominant strand in the narrative has been a belief in the current or impending impact of cataclysmic and immutable shifts in the nature of paid work – the end of careers as we know them, the rise in portfolio working, and, most importantly, the rise of the knowledge-driven economy and knowledge workers (Blair,

2007; Brown, 2007a; Leitch, 2005 and 2006). The bulk of the labour force either are, or will become, knowledge workers, or as Tony Blair put it, 'in a sense, a whole economy has passed away…In the new knowledge economy, human capital, the skills people possess, is critical' (Blair, 2007: 3). The persistence of low-paid, dead-end work has either been ignored, or it has been assumed that it can be tackled by upskilling those workers who fill these positions (see DCSF/DIUS, 2007 and LSC, 2007), though who would then occupy these jobs has never been vouchsafed. An associated belief has been that increasing wage inequality is the result of skill-biased technical change rather than, for example, the decline of collective bargaining (Leitch, 2005).

Because of the foregoing assumptions, the policy narrative suggests that both economic performance *and* social justice and mobility can best be served through improvements in the skill levels of individual workers (DIUS, 2007). As the Leitch Review's Final Report declared:

> *Our nation's skills are not world class and we run the risk that this will undermine the UK's long-term prosperity. Productivity continues to trail many of our main international comparators. Despite recent progress, the UK has serious social disparities with high levels of child poverty, poor employment rates for the disadvantaged, regional disparities and relatively high income inequality. Improving our skill levels can address all these problems.*

> (Leitch, 2006: 1)

This elision of individual and collective well-being (Ball, 2008: 17) was one of the main innovations injected into the narrative as it evolved under New Labour (see Keep and Mayhew, 2010 for a critique of this belief).

Crucially the narrative has argued that skills supply, not demand, is the central problem, with an explicit belief that if more skills are supplied, they will automatically be used, and productivity and economic competitiveness thereby enhanced. This is because supply is assumed (in a form of Say's Law) to create its own demand (what the Treasury term, a 'supply-push' effect, HMT, 2002). Grubb and Ryan dub this belief a 'build and they will come' myth (Grubb and Ryan, 1999).

The firm, policy has argued, is best treated as a black box into which inputs – such as enhanced skills and a better educated workforce – are injected, and from which will automatically emerge enhanced economic outcomes – greater productivity or higher value-added goods and services. Policy-makers do not need to know about what happens within the box (and hence the productive process) and it has normally been deemed illegitimate for policy to try to intervene within this 'sealed unit', as this is best left to management acting rationally in response to the invisible hand of market forces (Keep, 2002 and 2006b; Keep *et al.*, 2006).

It has, moreover, been assumed that learning is a uniform and uncomplicated process that can easily be managed through a simple input/output model. Coffield (2008) offers an extremely valuable discussion of the profound negative implications that have flowed from the adoption of this position by those designing and managing post-compulsory provision. In particular, he highlights the tendency for policy to obsess about the supportive infrastructure within the education and training system – strategies, targets, priorities, funding systems, performance management systems, inspection regimes, etc. – while 'the topics of teaching and learning disappear from sight, as if they had no momentum or dynamic of their own' (Coffield, 2008: 1).

Finally, under New Labour the narrative's authors were clear that the overriding goal of publicly-funded education and training ought to be to further economic aims and to boost competitiveness. Learning that sought to satisfy other, non-vocational needs came to be seen as being of much lesser importance, and public resources devoted to it were reduced to support more labour market-oriented forms of intervention (such as subsidised training delivered under Train to Gain[1] (National Audit Office, 2009)). As Coffield notes, what the Learning and Skills Council (LSC) termed 'learning for personal fulfilment, civic participation and community development' came to account for a tiny fraction of the overall post-19 budget (Coffield, 2008: 49).

The central conceptual pillars upon which the narrative has been founded can thus be seen to largely comprise simplified readings of human capital theory, market failure, and rate of return analyses – in other words, policy has been based on some relatively narrow elements of economic theory (Keep and Mayhew, 2010). One of the characteristics of the policy narrative has been the inability or unwillingness of its authors to assimilate, incorporate and learn from findings from the large body of international research on education and training and skills that has been generated over the last two decades on topics such as workforce development, and the links between skills and business strategies (Keep *et al.*, 2006; Keep, 2009). Examples of the narrow range of research material that makes its way into key policy documents would be the final report of the Leitch Review of Skills (Leitch, 2006), and the Analytical Paper produced in support of the Department for Business, Innovation and Skills' final skills strategy under New Labour (BIS, 2009).

Secondary elements

Besides these primary assumptions, the narrative has embraced and encoded a set of subsidiary, but extremely important, beliefs relating to the style and manner in which the English post-compulsory education and training system can best be designed and managed. The starting point has been a firm view that the centre knows best. Strategic policy formation should therefore usually be the sole preserve of ministers, advisors and senior civil servants – even within a system that at a rhetorical level has been said to be evidence-based, employer-led and student-centred. The choice of a set of policy levers or tools, such as marketisation, punitive inspection regimes and league tables, has both reflected and supported a belief that micro-management from the centre is both possible and indeed essential in order to deliver the government's plans and objectives (Coffield, 2008; Coffield *et al.*, 2008; Keep, 2009). Thus, one of the narrative's core functions has been to help coordinate and control priorities and policy thinking within what is one of the most centralised education and training systems in the Organisation for Economic Cooperation and Development (OECD) (Ainley, 2001). A wider discussion of the reasons for the tendency towards enhanced control from the centre is offered by Perry *et al.* (2010), and for general critiques of this model of governance and its consequences from within government itself, see Simon *et al.*, 2010; and National School of Government, 2009.

As a consequence of the above, the narrative has legitimised a disconnect between the few who make policy and the many who have to enact and deliver it on the ground (Coffield *et al.*, 2008) and the absence of what Coffield terms 'a democratic model of change' (2008: 2). The narrative demands centrally determined priorities, while eschewing any form of bottom-up feedback loops (see Chapter 6 for further reflections on this state of affairs).

As a result, the policy narrative has carried an explicit belief that power relationships are best managed in a top-down, command and control manner, and targets, set by the centre with minimal consultation, have been seen as the most appropriate way of driving the system, as, for example, those established by the Leitch Review (2006). The importance attached to management by target has had a profound impact on how the system is managed (see Coffield, 2008; and National School of Government, 2009), and what within it can be funded by government (it has to be measurable in simple units, e.g. a whole qualification). As a consequence, qualifications have been viewed as a good and sufficient proxy for skills and therefore as an ideal key performance indicator for the education and training system, even though research indicates that the vast bulk of skill formation inside the workplace is uncertified (see Keep, 2010a for further discussion of this point).

In general, the narrative has assumed a position that suggests that trust is a one-way street. Those at lower levels in the system must trust their superiors, while those in charge of the system normally cannot trust those at lower levels. This lack of trust has fed into a minimisation of the role of elected local government and its replacement by central government quangos and agencies, and also into a need for elaborate, top-down performance management systems and punitive forms of inspection regime (Coffield *et al.*, 2008). One reason for this approach has been the view by those at the centre of the system that FE colleges and private training providers are liable to be habitually unresponsive to their customers and hence continually in need of prodding, incentivising, berating, threatening, and performance managing in detail in order to make them undertake what is needed.

Besides targets, a key policy technology promoted within the narrative has been multi-layer skills forecasting and planning mechanisms, based around a simple matching model. One of the primary goals of policy, albeit a goal that has been very weakly specified at any level of detail (Keep, 2002, 2006b and 2010b) has been that of ensuring that the supply of publicly-funded education and training meets demand (whether from individuals, firms, sectors or occupations, across a range of differently specified geographic units). Thus local authorities via multi-area agreements, regional development agencies, sector skills councils, and the LSC and its successors (the Young People's Learning Agency and the Skills Funding Agency) have all been charged with trying to ensure that supply 'meets' demand (Denham, 2008).

The importance attached to the desirability of marketisation and contestability in education and training provision under the increasingly dominant New Public Management model (Perry *et al.*, 2010) has waxed and waned over time (Coffield *et al.*, 2008). During the last three years of the New Labour Administration (after the publication of the Leitch Review's final report in 2006) it became set on an upward curve, with plans for the opening up of almost the entire LSC £3 billion post-19 budget to contestability via routing funding through Train to Gain and Skills Accounts.

Finally, insofar as policy has ever been acknowledged to fail, the official belief is that it has done so because of failures of implementation and project management, not because of fundamental design flaws (Keep, 2006b and 2009). As senior ex-policy advisor Sir Michael Barber put it:

> *a lot of government programs start off with a good idea, but as they go through the bureaucracy and out into the system, compromises are made, and by the time it gets to the actual frontline, it is so watered down that it doesn't work. Then the frontline tells you the idea was bad when, actually, there was nothing wrong with the idea, just the implementation.*
>
> (Mead, 2006: 3)

This approach has helped ensure that few, if any, lessons have been learned from past policy failures.

These elements within the narrative have set the broad parameters for relationships between the centre and subordinate agencies and actors. It is important to note that the narrative has not been expected to rule out or to control the potential for overt or covert inter-agency rivalry or conflict. Nor has it been primarily focused on trying to define and dictate the detailed implementation of policy or the practice of delivery agents. What it has done has been to encode a set of basic beliefs that have justified and supported the continuity of the broad overall direction of strategy and high levels of resourcing, and as such has been but one weapon within a broader armoury of central control over the education and training system which includes government's powers of appointment and patronage (of not only agencies' managers, but also their councils and chairs); the honours system; the constant threat of disbandment of subordinate bodies; and control of funding, target-setting and inspection regimes (Keep, 2009).

Missing elements

As with most aspects of policy and its analysis, what is excluded is usually every bit as important as what is included. One of the central functions of the narrative has been to delineate those lines of policy development that are 'off limits' and thereby discourage or block any attempts to include them in official thinking or public debate. Topics, which in other developed countries (including those under conservative administrations, such as France and Germany) would often be seen as essential adjuncts to development of the education and training system, such as labour market regulation, collective bargaining arrangements and forms of education and training systems governance that embraced social partnership models, have all been absent. So too have been: the broader context of models of economic development that incorporate an active industrial policy; substantial efforts at economic development and business improvement; and the creation of patient and competent capital (a banking sector focused on long-term investment in native firms) (Keep et al., 2006; Keep, 2009; Keep and Mayhew, 2010). The lack of this second group of factors has reflected the fact that English skills policy has been explicitly designed to act as a partial substitute for these kinds of wider economic development policy instruments. They were deemed ideologically 'out of bounds' until the onset of the recession and the arrival of Lord Mandelson as Secretary of State at BIS prompted the start of a tentative rediscovery of industrial policy, or 'activism' (see below).

The narrative in operation

One way of conceiving of the narrative is that it has performed broadly the same functions as a church's creed and liturgy (Keep, 2009). It has set out the beliefs and values upon which policy and the activities that flow from policy are founded, and the forms and manner through which these beliefs are to be transmitted and reaffirmed. Within one of the most centralised education and training systems in the developed world it has also helped coordinate thinking, policy formation and action. It is the hymn sheet from which everyone learns to sing. It has thus had a very clear role in delineating the boundaries of what government and senior policy-makers believed was possible by way of lines of policy development, and in ensuring that those within the education and training system adopted, supported and operated within this 'assumptive universe' (for a much more detailed treatment of these issues, see Keep, 2009).

At the same time, the narrative has helped to provide policy with a relatively unchanging, central story across time. This has been a not unimportant function in an education and training system that has been subject to a loss of collective memory generated by turnover among ministers (Tuckett, 2008) and civil servants (Perry *et al.*, 2010), more or less ceaseless fluidity in the titles and policy borders of relevant central government departments, and even more frenetic changes among subordinate agencies and government education and training programmes, funding streams and qualifications structures (Stanton, 2009; Higham and Yeomans, 2007; Perry *et al.*, 2010). Some idea of the scale of this ceaseless organisational/structural revolution is provided in Chapter 5. All that will be noted here is that, of the education and training agencies that New Labour inherited in 1997, all but two (Ofsted and the Higher Education Funding Council for England) had been abolished or replaced by 2010. Casualties included national training organisations (NTOs), NTO National Council, training and enterprise councils (TECs), TEC National Council, the Further Education Funding Council for England, the LSC and local learning and skills councils, the Qualifications and Curriculum Authority, the Adult Learning Inspectorate, and a range of quality improvement bodies (see Coffield, 2008: 43).

The narrative has always been explicitly designed to be resistant to fundamental change and any attempt to reframe the skills policy 'problem' (Keep, 2006b and 2009). From the mid-1980s until the onset of the financial crisis in 2008 the narrative evolved through elaboration, but its fundamental direction and structure remained largely unaltered. The chief development was the tendency under the New Labour administrations for skills policy to bear an increasing set of expectations around social issues, such as poverty, income inequality and inter-generational social mobility (Keep, 2009; Keep and Mayhew, 2010).

Continuity or rupture?

The times they were a changin'…

Before the UK general election in 2010 it was becoming apparent that this previously fairly monolithic English policy narrative was coming under serious challenge on a number of fronts. First, the cumulative impact of research in the field of skills and its economic and social outcomes indicated ever more starkly that, on its own, enhancing levels of skills and qualifications only produced relatively limited outcomes, since the demand for skills within the economy was finite and relatively low, and skill utilisation often poor (Keep *et al.*, 2006; UKCES, 2009a; Keep and Mayhew, 2010). Research had also drawn attention to growing skill mismatches and levels of over-qualification (UKCES, 2009a).

Second, there had been an open abandonment of the traditional supply-led policy analysis in Scotland, and less overtly in Wales (see Chapters 3, 4 and 5 in this volume, plus Keep *et al.*, 2010b) – thereby demonstrating that alternative analyses and frames for policy action were possible within the overall UK political, economic and ideological environment. Developments in Scotland showed that the world does not collapse if you discard a simple strategy based around endless massification of education and training supply and move to a more balanced approach embracing the supply, demand and utilisation of skill (Scottish Government, 2007a and b) – for the story in Wales, see the Welsh Employment and Skills Board (WESB, 2009 and 2010). In addition, the Scottish experience demonstrated that highly centralised, top-down, low-trust control is not the only viable model for managing an education and training system, and that greater institutional autonomy, at both the level of government agency and individual education and training provider, does not necessarily lead to disaster.

Third, a combination of the two above-mentioned factors led the only UK-wide skills policy body – the UK Commission for Employment and Skills (UKCES) – to adopt a new analytical frame for policy and to embrace a substantially revised policy narrative that encompassed both a new meta-narrative (based around the demand for, supply of, and effective utilisation of skills; UKCES, 2009a) and notions of a simplified education and training system with higher levels of trust and lower levels of central control and management in detail (UKCES, 2008 and 2009b). In essence, the UKCES has acted as a mechanism, hitherto lacking, for comparing the merits of different policy approaches across the four countries of the UK and for then transmitting and disseminating the lessons of such comparisons and the new analytical frames they generate across the devolved national governments (see Keep *et al.*, 2010b).

Fourth, in the wake of the financial crisis and recession, a dawning occurred among some (but by no means all) senior English policy-makers, not least Lord Mandelson, that there were deep-seated structural imbalances in the economy and that a hands-off approach to economic development and the refusal to embrace any form of active industrial policy had left the UK/England facing significant problems around unemployment, occupational structures, income inequality, disparities in local and regional economic performance, innovation, investment and the balance of trade. The result was a belated rediscovery of issues concerning the demand side and the need for industrial strategies and national economic development policies (BIS, 2009). It should be stressed, however, that actual progress in coming to terms with what that might mean, or in beginning to develop policies in the light of this broader analysis, remained at a very early stage when the 2010 general election was called.

In addition, although the immediate effects were quite limited, the financial crisis, the recession and the impact of these events on the public finances, meant that, even if faith in the traditional supply-led model of skills policy had not been eroded, the resources to continue to support such an approach on the scale hitherto embraced were plainly unlikely to be available in future. After a decade of policy where money for new schemes, and an apparently endless ramping up of public support for existing forms of provision had been in ready supply, the party for education and training was suddenly seen to be over (see below).

All this suggests that the primary elements of the English policy narrative were coming under sustained pressure even before the general election. The arrival of a new government, and moreover a government that is a coalition of Liberal Democrat and Conservative parties and beliefs, plainly opens up the possibility for either revision to the *status quo ante*, or for further challenge to the narrative, and for its either partial reframing or total abandonment.

Given the changes in political and economic reality outlined above, an immediate question that presents itself is: what is liable to be the resultant political and ideological space and impetus for a rewriting of the policy narrative as it has hitherto existed? In answering this question, it is important to stress again that the narrative contains two separate but linked elements:

1. A 'big picture' story that explains what education and training policy is for and the range of economic and social ills which it can address.
2. A subordinate element that goes on to encode expectations about the form and manner of managerial arrangements whereby the education and training system is designed, funded, controlled and performance managed.

What follows will argue that change is more likely in the latter area than the former.

Change in subordinate elements of the narrative?

The model of highly centralised ministerial control, exercised through elaborate systems of national targets, subordinate funding agencies and inspection and quality improvement regimes that evolved under New Labour (Keep, 2002, 2006b, 2009; Coffield *et al.*, 2008; Coffield, 2008; Perry *et al.*, 2010) appears unlikely to be perpetuated in entirety in its old form under the Coalition Government. Involvement in meetings with the ministerial team at BIS leads the author to conclude that fewer targets, simpler and less directive funding systems, and greater institutional autonomy for colleges and training providers are liable to emerge as key elements in the future style of education and training governance. Echoes of this are to be found in the recent BIS (2010a) publication, *Skills for Sustainable Growth: Consultation on the future direction of skills policy*, and in key letters from ministers to the Association of Colleges (Gibb, 2010) and to the Association of Directors of Children's Services (Gove, 2010).

Such a development will necessitate the amendment of key elements of the old policy narrative to embrace notions of greater discretion and autonomy within the education and training system, and a more genuine partnership between central government and those on the ground who have to make policies work and deliver results. This will in turn require a profound cultural reorientation among civil servants and agency officials, who have grown used to superintending a culture of low-trust, top-down management. The difficulty of achieving this should not be under-estimated. The vast bulk of staff in central government and its agencies have spent their entire careers working within the 'assumptive world' created by the narrative in its current form, and some have been architects of the narrative, or elements therein (Keep, 2009). It, and the values and norms it embodies, are all they know and these represent a default 'world view' and a comfort zone that many may not be keen to leave.

For example, before the election UKCES (2009b) attempted to offer policy-makers a route to 'letting go' of detailed control of further education colleges and other providers, via a new performance management system, within which institutions could be judged but also given more discretion to act as they saw fit in meeting local needs. Unfortunately, while policy-makers adopted most of the form of the suggested amendments to the performance management regime (see BIS, 2009), they carefully watered down the implications of this change, in that a high degree of central control was to be maintained.

The other barrier to change is that spending cuts are liable to lead to greater competition for scarce resources between institutions and different streams of activity. In this context, providers are likely to become all the more anxious to be seen to be doing the government's bidding in the hope that this secures them favour, which in turn will secure them money. At the same time, from central government's point of view, with public money very tight, the tendency is liable to be to want to exert even greater detailed control over where, and how, and on what it is being spent.

The song remains the same…?

The case for continuity in the primary element of the narrative is, despite the change of government and the problems that the narrative was facing before the election, still surprisingly strong. To begin with, the Coalition

Conservative–Liberal Democrat Government faces many of the same ideological constraints as did its New Labour predecessor – a fact which speaks volumes about the element of neo-liberalism that lay at the heart of New Labour's political DNA.

In essence, as the author and others (Keep, 2002, 2006b, 2009; Keep *et al.*, 2010a; Keep and Mayhew, 2010) have argued, the importance attached to skills policy has occurred because it has offered, and continues to offer, one of the very few areas within the economy, societal relations and the labour market where government action has been deemed ideologically possible. Skills development has provided a legitimate tool for securing social and economic outcomes around topics such as enhanced productivity, social equity, poverty reduction and inter-generational social mobility. Because other forms of intervention have been politically 'off limits', skills policies have come to bear an increasingly heavy load of expectations and also to acquire an ever higher profile within the overall ambit of government policy. Thus, in the economic sphere, education and training and skills have appeared to offer the promise of 'intervention-free intervention' and a means by which government can boost economic performance without having to intervene inside the firm or try to exert direct influence over the competitive strategies of the private sector. In the social sphere, skills have appeared to hold out the even more enticing prospect of engendering 'loser-free redistribution' (Keep and Mayhew, 2010) whereby everyone can attain more rewarding and fulfilling employment through upskilling (Blair, 2007; Brown, 2007a and b). Such a belief flies in the face of a labour market where a high proportion of jobs (22 per cent) are low paid (Lloyd *et al.*, 2008), and where poor pay and job quality remain endemic (Lawton, 2009), but it has allowed government to avoid confronting issues around labour market regulation, class, gender and employee 'voice' and power (Keep and Mayhew, 2010).

The problem of ideological filtering, which leaves only a very narrowly circumscribed 'world of the possible' and hence an attenuated repertoire of alternative policy moves, is liable to be still more acute under the Coalition Government than it was under New Labour. Indeed it should be recalled that construction of the policy narrative was first commenced under the Conservative administrations of Mrs Thatcher and Mr Major. Skills development, along with concepts such as individual responsibility, freedom and enterprise, offer a 'get out of jail free' card for policy-makers of a Conservative/neo-liberal, Gladstonian/Liberal bent, when faced with deep-seated and apparently intractable structural problems within the fabric of the economy and society.

The key point is that it is relatively hard for government to design policy instruments and interventions that directly create responsibility, freedom or enterprise (or the spirit thereof), though of course they can try to adopt measures that will create an environment (economic and/or social) in which such virtues will spring to life. By contrast, it is relatively quick and easy to both enact and measure the delivery of certain forms of education and training activity and of skills (Perry *et al.*, 2010). Thus the government can be seen to be 'doing something' direct and concrete about tackling pressing social and economic ills, and ministers are able to launch initiatives and announce reforms that give the impression of purpose and dynamism.

The main elements of the Government's economic policies as announced so far suggest that the traditional skills policy narrative around the need for more and better education and training can carry on, albeit now somewhat watered down in terms of public support, but garbed afresh with new rhetoric – enterprise, freedom, standards, traditional values, markets and choice all seem likely candidates for inclusion or greater stress within the new policy vocabulary. The old narrative seems to fit in quite well, if economic policy revolves, as early indications appear to suggest, around the somewhat familiar tropes of fiscal rectitude; liberalisation and de-regulation; low levels of business taxation; rejigged regional and local economic development; and supply-side interventions around skills, publicly-funded research and development, the transport infrastructure and banking reform (Osborne, 2010; Cameron, 2010; BIS, 2010b) – most of which were staples of policy throughout most of New Labour's period in office. Indeed, David Cameron's first speech as Prime Minister on the future shape of the economy (Cameron, 2010) mentioned schools and training for young people as key elements of the support that the Government wants to offer to get the economy into better shape.

The space for change and amendment of the narrative appears to centre on what Vince Cable and BIS want, and are able to create, by way of wider conceptions of policies aimed at 'supporting growing industries' (Cameron, 2010), though early indications are (BIS, 2010b) that the policy cupboard is fairly bare of new initiatives and may contain nothing substantively different from that stocked by its New Labour predecessors. New ways of thinking might, for example, stretch as far as activity that could begin to address the weakness of skill utilisation in the economy – a policy area where hitherto Scotland has made all the running in the UK (see Chapter 3).

However, the ability to justify government interventions in this area in ideological terms that can win the support of politicians and civil servants is not going to be at all easy. Until the recession and the then Government's belated rediscovery of industrial policy, it was not regarded as acceptable territory for policy development under New Labour, and for some indication of the current sensitivity of the topic one need look no further than the recent report from UKCES on high performance working (UKCES, 2010a), which tiptoes around the topic of workplace skill utilisation as though walking on eggshells. The simple reality is that in most other European countries, whatever the political orientation of their governments, there are, and have been for a long time, concerted programmes of public support aimed at fostering workplace innovation, quality of working life and higher workplace productivity (see Ramstad, 2009a and b for details). In England, even discussing such programmes, never mind suggesting that they be replicated here, is still apparently hugely problematic for policy-makers.

In the longer term, the ability to sustain the 'skills as an answer to economic and social weaknesses' story faces a fundamental problem. This comes in the shape of the impending cuts in public expenditure. These will almost certainly further expose and exacerbate the gap between official ambitions, targets and aspirations, and the public and private resources available to meet them (see, for example, UKCES, 2009a and 2010b, on faltering progress towards the targets set by the Leitch Review). Within an ideological settlement that has always dictated expanded public provision coupled with a largely voluntarist system of employer training, the ability to mandate employers to take action, to provide training or to be required to co-fund education and training activity to match government expenditure has always been very limited. The policy narrative, therefore, always centred on the ability of government to step in and either directly provide what was lacking (through expansion of post-compulsory provision) or latterly through different forms of subsidy to employers (for example, Train to Gain). The suggestion has always been that state spending will either leverage in voluntary employer contributions, which in the case of Train to Gain it manifestly failed to achieve at anything like the expected level (Ofsted, 2008; National Audit Office, 2009); or that a publicly-funded 'supply push' would, as noted above, ultimately catalyse a transformation of employers' product market strategies and hence deliver a step change in the demand for skills (HMT, 2002). Leaving aside the fact that neither expectation was supported by experience, a state-led drive towards 'world class' ambitions around skill levels (Leitch, 2006) is no longer likely to be possible on the same scale because the money to support it has vanished. At a stroke, one of the major supporting mechanisms for the narrative has been gravely weakened. The key question will be how policy-makers choose to react to these straitened circumstances.

In essence, policy-makers are liable to find themselves caught between conflicting requirements. On the one hand, given that the ideological 'no go' zones that exist for the new Coalition Government are even more extensive than they were for New Labour, the need to deploy skills as an ideologically acceptable economic and social cure-all remains very strong. On the other, sharply diminished public funding, coupled with an inability to compel employers to do more, means that the gap between ambitions for education and training and what is actually delivered is liable to grow. Given the strong ideological unpalatability of the other possible policy approaches to tackling existing economic and social weaknesses, the likelihood is that government will simply quietly water down or abandon some of the targets and ambitions that it has inherited in the skills area, overlay some new language and slogans onto the traditional skills narrative, and hope for the best. Skills policy may prove, once again, unable to deliver what has been promised in terms of economic success and social justice, but even if this is the case, it serves a vital function in helping to hide the absence of other policy approaches that might make headway in these areas.

Final thoughts

Given the immediate pressures generated by budget reduction, cuts in public spending and doubtless the media 'noise' generated by policy moves around academies, 'free' schools and student fees and/or graduate tax in HE, it will take time for a clear direction of travel for broader education and training policy to emerge. This chapter has outlined one path that policy might take. Whether this will be chosen is unclear at this juncture, but it appears likely that the policy narrative will undergo some reshaping in order to nuance it to meet straitened circumstances and new expectations.

Perhaps the key issue will be whether the new Government finds itself willing and able to open up the future direction of policy to any real public debate that might include stakeholders such as employers, unions, education and training institutions and deliverers and their staff, and the research community. As noted above, one of the functions of the policy narrative has been to limit the space for any such debate of the fundamental assumptions, functions and direction of policy to take place. If such a development is not forthcoming, the likelihood is that policy, and the explanatory narrative that underlies it, will carry on along broadly the same tramlines as before, albeit with fewer resources but with some new rhetorical embellishments. Thus it will again be a case of policy seeking 'more of the same, for less, forever'.

If the UK Government does choose to take this path of least innovation (and hence least resistance), then the gap between its education and training and skills policies and those being pursued in Scotland and Wales will almost inevitably continue to widen. The Scots in particular are evolving a radically different policy narrative, which embraces the need for policy interventions that simultaneously address the supply of, demand for, and utilisation of skills (Scottish Government, 2007a and b), which deploys a different model of performance management, and which embraces levels of institutional autonomy and grassroots innovation that would be unthinkable in England.

Note

1   Train to Gain was devised as a government programme that offered employers state subsidy to support certain types of training, e.g. adult literacy and numeracy, and achievement of whole qualifications (almost always National Vocational Qualifications) primarily at Levels 2 and 3 for workers without a first Level 2 or 3 qualification. Subsidy was to be channelled via a network of independent training brokers who would offer the employer a choice of providers (public and private) that could meet their training needs. After the Leitch Review (Leitch, 2006) the Government decided that the entire post-19 education and training budget allocated to support employer training would be directed via Train to Gain. Subsequently, although the Train to Gain brand has been maintained, the range of training it will support has been extended to include apprenticeships, while the levels of funding for Level 2 and 3 training for adult workers have been scaled back.

    Skills Accounts were proposed by the Leitch Review as a means of enhancing contestability between education and training providers for all forms of government support available post-19 to individual learners. Almost the whole of the post-19 budget for individual learners (outside of higher education provision) was planned to be channelled through such accounts. The 'account' is notional (the individual does not receive the actual money, but is given information on what s/he is entitled to). The account will only fund certain types of learning, chosen by government.

References

Ainley, P. (2001) 'From a national system locally administered to a national system nationally administered: The new leviathan in education and training'. *Journal of Social Policy*, 30(3), 457–76.

Ball, S.J. (2008) *The Education Debate*. Bristol: Policy Press.

Blair, A. (2007) 'Our nation's future: The role of work'. <www.number-10.gov.uk/output/Page11405.asp> (accessed 4 May 2007).

Blunkett, D. (2001*) Education into Employability: The role of the DfEE in the economy*. Sudbury: Department for Education and Employment.

Brown, G. (2007a) 'Speech to the CBI: 26 November'. <http://www.number10.gov.uk/output/Page13851.asp> (accessed 28 November 2007).

-- (2007b) 'Speech on education: 31 October 2007'. <http://www.number10.gov.uk/output/Page13675.asp> (accessed 29 November 2007).

Cameron, D. (2010) 'Transforming the British Economy: Coalition strategy on economic growth'. 28 May. <http://www.conservatives.com/News/Speeches/2010/05/David_Cameron_Transforming_the_British_economy.aspx> (accessed 27 October 2010).

Coffield, F. (2008) *Just Suppose Teaching and Learning became the First Priority...* London: Learning and Skills Network.

Coffield, F., Edward, S., Finlay, I., Hodgson, A., Spours, K. and Steer, R. (2008) *Improving Learning, Skills and Inclusion: The impact of policy on post-compulsory education*. London: Routledge/Falmer.

Denham, J. (2008) 'Strategic Skills: Right skills, right place, right time', speech to the Confederation of British Industry (CBI). London, 24 October. <http://nationalemployerservice.org.uk/resources/strategic-skills-right-skills-right-place-right-time/> (accessed 27 October 2010).

Department for Business, Innovation and Skills (BIS) (2009) *Skills for Growth: The national skills strategy*. Cm 7641. London: The Stationery Office.

-- (2010a) *Skills for Sustainable Growth: Consultation on the future direction of skills policy*. June. London: BIS.

-- (2010b) *A Strategy for Sustainable Growth*. London: BIS.

Department for Children, Schools and Families/Department for Innovation, Universities and Skills (DCSF/DIUS)(2007) 'LSC Grant Letter: 2008–09' (mimeo). London: DCSF.

Department for Education and Employment (DfEE) (1998) *The Learning Age: A renaissance for a new Britain*. London: HMSO.

Department for Education and Skills (DfES) (2004*) Department for Education and Skills: Five year strategy for children and learners*. Cm 6272. London: HMSO.

Department for Education and Skills/Department for Trade and Industry/HM Treasury/Department for Work and Pensions (2005) *Skills: Getting on in business, getting on in work*. Cm 6483. London: HMSO.

Department for Education and Skills/HM Treasury/Department for Trade and Industry/Department for Work and Pensions (2003*) 21st Century Skills: Realising our potential: individuals, employers, nation*. Cm 5810. London: HMSO.

Department for Innovation, Universities and Skills (DIUS) (2007) *World Class Skills: Implementing the Leitch Review of Skills in England*. Cm 7181. London: HMSO.

-- (2008) *Higher Education at Work – High skills: high value*. London: DIUS.

Gibb, N. (2010) *Letter to Mr Martin Doel, Association of Colleges*. 19 July. London: Department for Education (DfE).

Gove, M. (2010) *Letter to Marion Davis, President of the Association of Directors of Children's Services*. London: DfE.

Grubb, W.N. (2004) 'The Anglo-American approach to vocationalism: The economic roles of education in England'. *SKOPE Research Paper* No. 52. Coventry: University of Warwick, The ESRC Centre on Skills, Knowledge and Organisational Performance (SKOPE).

Grubb, W.N. and Lazerson, M. (2004) *The Education Gospel: The economic power of schooling*. Cambridge, MA: Harvard University Press.

Grubb, W.N. and Ryan, P. (1999) *The Roles of Evaluation for Vocational Education and Training*. London: International Labour Office/Kogan Page.

Her Majesty's Treasury (HMT) (2002) *Developing Workforce Skills: Piloting a new approach*. London: HMT.

Higham, J. and Yeomans, D. (2007) 'Policy memory and policy amnesia in 14–19 education: Learning from the past?'. In D. Raffe and K. Spours (eds), *Policy-making and Policy Learning in 14–19 Education*. London: Institute of Education, University of London, 33–60.

Keep, E. (2002) 'The English vocational education and training debate: Fragile "technologies" or opening the "black box": two competing visions of where we go next'. *Journal of Education and Work*, 15(4), 457–79.

-- (2006a) 'Market failure in skills'. *SSDA Catalyst*, 1. Wath-upon-Dearne: Sector Skills Development Agency.

-- (2006b) 'State control of the English education and training system: Playing with the biggest trainset in the world'. *Journal of Vocational Education and Training*, 58(1), 47–64.

-- (2008) 'From competence and competition to the Leitch Review: The utility of comparative analyses of skills and performance'. *IES Working Paper* No. 14. Brighton: Institute of Employment Studies.

-- (2009) 'The limits of the possible: Shaping the learning and skills landscape through a shared policy narrative'. *SKOPE Research Paper* No. 86. Cardiff: Cardiff University, SKOPE.

-- (2010a) 'Recent research on workplace learning and its implications for national skills policies across the OECD'. In J. Bryson (ed.), *Beyond Skill: Institutions, organisations and human capability*. London: Palgrave Macmillan, 105–26.

-- (2010b) 'The challenges and dilemmas of public skills policy and investment'. In *Foresight: Skills*. Cambridge: East of England Development Agency.

Keep, E. and Mayhew, K. (2010) 'Moving beyond skills as a social and economic panacea?'. *Work, Employment and Society*, 24(3), 1–15.

Keep, E., Lloyd, C. and Payne, J. (2010a) 'The elephant in the corner: Skills policy and the displacement of industrial relations'. In T. Colling and M. Terry (eds), *Industrial Relations: Theory and practice*, 4th edition. Oxford: Blackwell, 398–421.

Keep, E., Mayhew, K. and Payne, J. (2006) 'From skills revolution to productivity miracle: Not as easy as it sounds?'. *Oxford Review of Economic Policy*, 22(4), 539–59.

Keep, E., Mayhew, K., Payne, J. and Stasz, C. (eds) (2008) *Education, Skills and the Economy: The politics of vocational education and training*. Cheltenham: Edward Elgar.

Keep, E., Payne, J. and Rees, G. (2010b) 'Devolution and strategies for learning and skills: The Leitch Report and its alternatives'. In G. Lodge and K. Schmuecker (eds), *Devolution in Practice 2010*. London: Institute of Public Policy Research, 83–100.

Lawton, K. (2009) *Nice Work If You Can Get It*. London: Institute of Public Policy Research.

Learning and Skills Council (LSC) (2001) *Learning and Skills Council Strategic Framework to 2004 Corporate Plan*. Coventry: LSC.

-- (2005) *Planning for Success: A framework for planning and quality*. Coventry: LSC.

-- (2007) *Our Statement of Priorities. Better skills, better jobs, better lives: The Learning and Skills Council's priorities and key actions for 2008/09 to 2010/11*. Coventry: LSC.

Leitch Review of Skills (2005) *Skills in the UK: The long-term challenge*. Interim Report. London: HM Treasury.

-- (2006) *Prosperity for All in the Global Economy: World class skills*. Final report. London: HM Treasury.

Lloyd, C., Mason, G. and Mayhew, K. (eds) (2008) *Low-Wage Work in the United Kingdom*. New York: Russell Sage Foundation.

Mead, S. (2006) 'Education reform lessons from England, an interview with Sir Michael Barber'. Education Sector Interviews, EducationSector, <http://www.educationsector.org/publications/education-reform-lessons-england> (accessed 27 October 2010).

National Audit Office (NAO) (2009) *Train to Gain: Developing the skills of the workforce*. HC 879 Session 2008–09. London: NAO.

National School of Government (2009) *Engagement and Aspiration: Reconnecting policy making with front line professionals*. London: Cabinet Office.

Office for Standards in Education, Children's Services and Skills (Ofsted) (2008) *The Impact of Train to Gain on Skills in Employment*. Reference No. 070250. London: Ofsted.

Osborne, G. (2010) 'Speech by the Chancellor of the Exchequer, the Rt Hon George Osborne MP, at the CBI Annual Dinner, Grosvenor House Hotel, London'. <www.hm-treasury.gov.uk/speech_chx_190510.htm> (accessed 24 May 2010).

Perry, A., Amadeo, C., Fletcher, M. and Walker, E. (2010) 'Instinct or reason: How education policy is made and how we might make it better'. *CfBT Education Trust Perspective Report*. London: CfBT Education Trust/Learning and Skills Network.

Ramstad, E. (2009a) 'Promoting performance and the quality of working life simultaneously'. *International Journal of Productivity and Performance Management*, 58(5), 423–36.

-- (2009b) 'Expanding innovation system and policy: An organisational perspective'. *Policy Studies*, 30(5), 533–53.

Scottish Government (2007a) *Skills for Scotland: A lifelong skills strategy*. Edinburgh: Scottish Government.

-- (2007b) *The Government Economic Strategy*. Edinburgh: Scottish Government.

Simon, P., Paun, A., McClory, J. and Blatchford, K. (2010) *Shaping Up: A Whitehall for the future*. London: Institute for Government.

Stanton, G. (2009) *Learning Matters: Making the 14–19 reforms work for learners*. Reading: CfBT Education Trust.

Tuckett, A. (2008) 'We can't afford to lose all our adult learners'. *Education Guardian*, 15 January, 8.

UK Commission for Employment and Skills (UKCES) (2008) *Simplification of Skills in England: Expert advice to government on simplification of the English post-compulsory skills system for employers*. Wath-upon-Dearne: UKCES.

-- (2009a) *Towards Ambition 2020: Skills, jobs and growth*. Wath-upon-Dearne: UKCES.

-- (2009b) *Hiding the Wiring: Final assessment of progress on implementing the recommendations in Simplification of Skills in England*. Wath-upon-Dearne: UKCES.

-- (2010a) *High Performance Working: A policy review*. UKCES Evidence Report No. 18. Wath-upon-Dearne: UKCES.

-- (2010b) *Ambition 2020: The 2010 report*. Wath-upon-Dearne: UKCES.

Welsh Employment and Skills Board (WESB) (2009) *A Wales That Works*. Cardiff: WESB.

-- (2010) *Moving Forward: Foundations for Growth. Volume 1, Economic Renewal and the Skills Agenda*. Cardiff: WESB.

Chapter 3

The Scottish perspective: Continuity and change post-devolution

Janet Lowe and Vernon Gayle

The policy context prior to devolution

Scotland had its own distinctive education and training systems long before devolution (Byrne and Raffe, 2005). Its institutions and qualifications systems have evolved separately from those of the other 'home' nations; and the administration of education and training was largely devolved to the Scottish Office well before political devolution in 1999. However, there are also strong interdependencies between Scotland and England, particularly in the post-school sectors, which operate within the UK labour market and which are subject to UK-wide policies in employment and social security (Rees, 2002). There are common economic and social discourses within the UK and internationally, which elicit convergent responses in the way that policy is developed and implemented and which have had an impact both before and after devolution in 1999.

In the late 1990s, the educational policy environment throughout the UK was characterised by an explicit acceptance of the importance of moving towards lifelong learning and a learning society. Researchers sought to understand the concept of a learning society in economic, social and democratic terms, defining a learning society as one 'which would combine excellence with equity and would equip all its citizens with the knowledge, understanding and skills to ensure national economic prosperity and much more besides' (Coffield, 1997: 450). In policy terms, *The Learning Age: Renaissance for a new Britain* (DfEE, 1998) reflected and built upon the Kennedy (1997) and Fryer (1997) reports, both of which advocated widening access to, and participation in, lifelong learning in order to deliver economic success and social cohesion. In Scotland, the Secretary of State for Scotland similarly published a Green Paper on lifelong learning, *Opportunity Scotland* (Scottish Office, 1998), which set the ambitious goal that, by 2002, all Scottish citizens would have the means to access lifelong learning at any stage of their lives.

These policy statements are set within a discourse of a changing world and a shift to knowledge as the basis of value creation in the economy. Lifelong learning was believed to be crucial to enabling the UK and Scotland to respond to the anticipated political, economic, industrial, social and technological changes flowing from the emerging global knowledge economy. *Opportunity Scotland* notably asserts that learning is also a vital element of a successful, healthy, vibrant and democratic society. Policy statements appear to accept unquestioningly that lifelong learning and a learning society will contribute to economic success, social justice, competitiveness, prosperity, sustained employment and quality of life (Tight, 1998).

The rhetoric is not, however, converted into a radical, strategic plan to implement the vision of a learning society. Instead, there is an assumption that progress towards lifelong learning is somehow inevitable and that it therefore represents a context in which specific, mainly vocational, lifelong learning policy initiatives should be pursued, primarily aimed at driving up participation among sometimes unwilling 'conscripts' (Tight, 1998).

The Scottish Parliament and the Scottish Executive: 1999–2007

From 1999, we can consider how policy on lifelong learning in Scotland continued to evolve through the work of the Scottish Parliament, which assumed fully devolved responsibility for education in Scotland in 1999. For the first two four-year terms of the Parliament from 1999 to 2007, the Government was a coalition between the Labour and Liberal Democrat parties (the Government and its administration was known as the Scottish Executive). From 2007, a Scottish National Party (SNP) minority government came to power (the administration was re-badged as the Scottish Government). These two periods of devolved government will be considered separately because there are clear distinctions between the two.

The Scottish Executive's (1999) first programme for government, *Making it Work Together*, incorporated many of the themes of *Opportunity Scotland*, by including commitments to provide training for skills that match jobs for the future, to widen access to further and higher education, to create a culture of lifelong learning and to increase adult participation in education and training. 'Skills' and 'lifelong learning' were brought together under a common theme of 'enterprise', but were accorded distinct purposes and objectives, arguably because there were, and would continue to be, separate funding streams for, respectively, national training programmes and further and higher education. The second programme for government, *Working Together for Scotland*, published when Henry McLeish replaced Donald Dewar as First Minister, aimed for a 'highly skilled, learning, earning, connected Scotland', 'making a reality of the promise of lifelong learning, learning today for the jobs of tomorrow' (Scottish Executive, 2001a: 17). These broad statements of intent were supported by policy documents, which are considered later in this chapter, and by the appointment of a minister and the establishment of a government department for Enterprise, Transport and Lifelong Learning, separated from school education.

Although this may appear to foreshadow a shift towards a more economic perspective on lifelong learning, both the Parliament and the Executive retained a broad view of the purpose of skills and lifelong learning as essential for both economic development and social inclusion. The new Scottish Executive created a plethora of new bodies charged with implementing aspects of the government programme, including the Scottish Further Education Funding Council; the Scottish University for Industry and Learndirect Scotland, which were tasked with stimulating demand for lifelong learning;[1] Future Skills Scotland, which was created to generate and publish labour market information;[2] Careers Scotland, a new 'all-age' careers guidance service;[3] and an infrastructure to lead the implementation of the Scottish Credit and Qualifications Framework.[4] The launch or reorganisation of agencies and initiatives created an impression of activity and progress with the emphasis clearly on increasing participation in adult lifelong learning. There does not appear to be any overall strategic intent to change the systems of post-16 education nor a recognition of the political, financial and institutional implications of shifting towards an accessible system of lifelong learning for people of all ages. In particular, separate funding streams were, and would continue to be, retained for vocational skills training and for further education.

The first two terms of the Scottish Parliament were politically turbulent, with three successive First Ministers and no less than six ministers with responsibility for lifelong learning, drawn from both coalition partners. Not surprisingly, this resulted in the publication of policy statements on skills and lifelong learning from different perspectives and perhaps in part contributed to a proliferation of new initiatives, projects and funding streams, as ministers sought to highlight the role and value of the new Parliament to the people of Scotland.

The period 2001–2003 saw the Scottish Parliament and the Scottish Executive develop differentiated approaches to setting policy in lifelong learning and in higher education through a series of Inquiries by the Parliament (Scottish Parliament, 2002, 2003), reviews by the Executive into higher education (Scottish Executive, 2003a, 2004) and publication of policy documents by ministers (Scottish Executive, 2003b, 2003c). Parliamentary committees were new in Scotland and they were keen to be active. Inquiries promoted civic engagement through extensive evidence-gathering sessions and enabled researchers to present findings and influence the debate. The Enterprise and Lifelong Learning Committee's Inquiry into Lifelong Learning (Scottish Parliament, 2002) adopted an inclusive approach to lifelong learning, taking as its field of inquiry: higher education, further education, vocational learning, community and voluntary education. The Committee advocated the preparation of a national lifelong learning strategy, the aim of which would be: 'to create a culture where everyone has the desire and opportunity to continuously develop their knowledge and skills, thus enhancing their quality of life and the well being of society' (Scottish Parliament, 2002: 15).

The Committee's report (2002) adopted the familiar rhetoric of learning as crucially important for economic success, social justice and citizenship, but went on to advocate some radical changes. The Committee concluded that vocational training, higher education, further education, community and voluntary education should no longer be treated as separate sectors but rather as part of a lifelong learning system. The Committee recommended progress towards a single, cohesive system underpinned by a standard basic entitlement to lifelong learning available to every citizen. They recommended a single funding system, and the equalisation of fee support for full-time and part-time learners. The Committee made the obvious observation that the expansion of part-time learning would be essential for a culture of lifelong learning and that inequitable differentiation between financial support for full-time and part-time learners was likely to be stifling demand.

A parliamentary committee that does not have the power and burden of policy implementation was able to be more strategic and systemic in its conclusions. It is perhaps then disappointing to conclude that little, if any, direct change emerged as a result of its deliberations. We observe that none of the inquiries and reviews undertaken during the first term of the new Parliament resulted in any significant change, with the notable exception of the Review of Student Finance (Cubie, 1999), which paved the way for the abolition of tuition fees for full-time higher education in Scotland.

Scottish Executive policy for lifelong learning and skills

In parallel with the inquiries and reviews, two policy statements entered the public arena. Both are strong on rhetoric, light on strategy and seek change through new agencies and initiatives. Wendy Alexander, as Minister for Enterprise and Lifelong Learning, led the development of *A Smart, Successful Scotland* (Scottish Executive, 2004), which articulated, for the first time, a clear vision for the role of skills and learning 'at the heart of our economic development services'. *A Smart, Successful Scotland* was directed at the operation of Scotland's two Enterprise Networks: Scottish Enterprise; and Highlands and Islands Enterprise. As such, its scope was constrained, particularly in relation to skills, as the Networks had limited budgets (about £120 million per annum) for skills interventions. Nevertheless, this is a rare example of an holistic skills and economic development strategy in which the contribution of skills to improvements in productivity and economic growth is presented alongside, although not necessarily well integrated with, business development interventions. The specific skills interventions that were set out were restricted to a range of already existing training measures particularly for young people (this is what the budgets were used for), but there was a shift in the perceived purpose of these programmes. Prior to *A Smart, Successful Scotland*, national training programmes were viewed primarily as palliatives to address youth and adult unemployment. In contrast, *A Smart, Successful Scotland* proposed that skills training should underpin improved economic performance.

In 2003 a new Minister, Iain Gray, published *Life Through Learning Through Life* (Scottish Executive, 2003b), which is located within the wider discourse on lifelong learning, combined with a series of tactical initiatives. *Life Through Learning Through Life* sets out a five-year strategy based on a new vision of lifelong learning in Scotland as 'the best possible match between the learning opportunities open to people and the skills, knowledge, attitudes and behaviours which will strengthen Scotland's economy and society' (Scottish Executive, 2003b: 6). Lifelong learning is defined as being 'about personal fulfilment and enterprise; employability and adaptability; active citizenship and social inclusion' (Scottish Executive, 2003b: 7).

The concept of lifelong learning encompasses all of post-compulsory education, training and learning. Two challenges are identified from an analysis of the socio-economic context: first, low productivity and low economic growth in Scotland compared to some other advanced countries; and second, a projected decline in the working-age population.

The proposed solution to these challenges was to establish a healthy, sustainable and flexible labour market, through increased participation in lifelong learning. There is no clear explanation of the rationale for the assumption that increased participation in learning will increase the flexibility of the labour market, which will, in turn, address the two identified challenges. Although *Life Through Learning Through Life* acknowledged the report of the Parliament's Enterprise and Lifelong Learning Committee (2002), it declined to adopt the more radical agenda that the Committee had proposed. Instead, the tactical initiatives proposed throughout the document are designed either to improve the quality and responsiveness of the supply of learning opportunities and/or to increase participation. They represent a motley collection of existing and new interventions. Examples include Individual Learning Accounts, more places in colleges, more Apprenticeships, Educational Maintenance

Allowances, the Scottish Union Learning Fund, school–college partnerships, Enterprise Education, Adult Literacy projects and Public Internet Access Points. The six indicators against which progress would be measured all relate to participation rates and levels of qualifications within the population.

Life Through Learning Through Life continues to exemplify ambiguity about the relationship, in Scotland, between 'skills', generally taken to mean national training programmes managed by the Enterprise Networks, and 'lifelong learning', generally taken to mean all other post-school learning provision except higher education. Informed readers of the two documents perceived that they represented, respectively, the balance between Scotland's twin goals of economic competitiveness (represented by *A Smart, Successful Scotland*) and social inclusion and personal fulfilment (represented by *Life Through Learning Through Life)* (Byrne and Raffe, 2005). The latter does include cross-references to the former and to the economic development role of skills, but it also then incorporates a strong economic purpose for lifelong learning. Indeed, the two challenges that the strategy sets out to address are primarily economic in nature. *Life Through Learning Through Life* also announced plans for the merger of the Scottish Further Education Funding Council and the Scottish Higher Education Funding Council, a merger that would also create the new Council's Skills Committee, further blurring the distinction between skills and post-school education. A planned review of funding for learners was also proposed. There is, however, no evidence of an appetite for considering the system of post-school learning as a whole and no evidence of interest in a more strategic approach to the prioritisation of resource allocation.

The role of colleges

This review of policy has painted a picture of tactical rather than strategic change in the implementation of policy goals for lifelong learning and skills. Perhaps the exception to that is the significant shift in the government's relationship with colleges and their role in policy implementation, which took place post-1997. During the period of the Conservative Government prior to 1997, colleges had been withdrawn from local authority control and incorporated as independent organisations in their own right. Incorporation was followed by a punishing drive towards efficiency, through incentivising colleges to compete for resources during a period when the amount available for distribution was being reduced in real terms (McTavish, 2003). The arrival of the Labour Government in 1997 and the Scottish Parliament in 1999 heralded a more benign political environment for colleges, in which collaboration rather than competition was encouraged, and a period of increased resources. The Comprehensive Spending Review in Scotland delivered additional funding of 50 per cent over the life of the first Scottish Parliament (Scottish Executive,

2001b), creating a context for colleges to gain confidence, visibility and influence in the policy agenda.

Colleges, individually and collectively, took up this opportunity and embarked on a period of sustained and growing influence in shaping policy rather than serving as delivery agents. This was underpinned by the merger of the former further and higher education funding councils, a development that further strengthened the colleges' position in the post-school system. It could be argued that a relative lack of centrally driven strategic direction in policy implementation, combined with increased resources, created space for innovation and change in institutions such as colleges in Scotland, with positive benefits at local and regional level – a context that the next government would inherit and use to its advantage.

1999–2007: Summary

In 2006, under yet another new Minister, Nichol Stephen, the Scottish Executive produced *Strategy Update* (Scottish Executive, 2006) outlining progress against the goals of *Life Through Learning Through Life*. This would be the last in a series of progress reports against the targets set in the original document. It represents the Government's analysis of what had improved in three years. An alternative and more cynical interpretation might suggest complacency.

Strategy Update concluded that Scotland's skilled workforce was a key economic strength; that the population was motivated, skilled and willing to learn; that participation levels were high; that the education and training system was working well and delivering what employers needed; that employers were investing in their staff; that the policy environment was working well; and that the increasing demand for high skills could be met. Almost all of the measures and the quantitative indicators that are presented in evidence are supply-side measures and, on closer inspection, several of the indicators reveal recent progress in the wrong direction.[5] There was little attempt to analyse whether Scotland was better prepared to address the challenges of economic growth and demographic change.

Strategy Update does acknowledge that some difficulties remain to be overcome. These are, however, defined only in terms of failure to participate in lifelong learning on the part of young people not in education, employment or training (NEETs) and low-skilled workers. The *Strategy Update* also documents the future implications of a declining cohort of young people entering the labour market. Ever-increasing participation is seen, rather simplistically, as the only remaining policy priority.

In summary, during the first two terms of the Scottish Parliament, from 1999–2007, the Scottish Executive tended to align with the UK rhetoric that driving up participation in lifelong learning through investment in the supply of provision would lead to a more successful knowledge economy. This was balanced, particularly in Scotland, by a parallel conviction that a strong economy and a strong society were two sides of the same coin and that lifelong learning had a vital role to play in underpinning social justice and citizenship. The Scottish Parliament appeared to be prepared to take a more far-reaching approach to recommending systemic change, but the Scottish Executive's policy statements stopped short of strategic plans for reforming the whole system. Instead there is evidence of a proliferation of new agencies, reviews and initiatives. The impression gained is one of almost frantic effort to bring about change through a patchwork of loosely related initiatives. We argue that a belief in the importance and inevitability of a culture of lifelong learning, combined with the quantum of policy activity, masked a lack of clarity about the rationale for change and about how change was to be brought about. The underlying problem was almost always defined as under-participation, and the primary objectives were therefore to drive up demand by increasing supply through investment in more of the same provision. The period ended with a remarkable complacency about the effectiveness of the interventions.

2007: Election of a Scottish National Party Government

The outcome of the 2007 Scottish Parliamentary election was the formation of a minority SNP government. As a nationalist administration, the SNP would set out to develop a distinctive direction for Scotland and, as a minority administration, would have more limited scope to achieve change through legislation. Added to this was a sense of urgency and determination to progress towards a very clear political goal and a more cohesive political leadership than had been possible for a coalition government.

The new Government began with an analysis of the context that it had inherited and formed a more negative, and arguably more realistic, view of social and economic life in contemporary Scotland (Scottish Government, 2007a). The analysis concluded that Scotland's economy had underperformed for decades, with poorer productivity and lower participation rates than comparators in the UK and further afield. There had also been net out-migration and lower population growth, combined with persistent social and economic inequalities. The Government accepted its predecessor administration's positive assessment of the skills of the workforce and acknowledged that the population was well qualified, and that participation in post-school learning was high. Indeed, as the Leitch Review of Skills confirmed, Scotland is the only nation or region of the United Kingdom where the percentage of people with a higher education qualification outnumbers the percentage with a basic school-leaving qualification (Leitch, 2005, 2006). Compared with other areas of the UK, Scotland ranks third in terms of the percentage of the population with a degree-level qualification or above; and in terms of the population with up to SCQF Level 9[6] qualification or above, Scotland ranks second. The Scottish Government also acknowledged that the post-school education system appeared to be working well. There was, therefore, *prima facie* evidence of effective investment in skills within Scotland. However, the analysis went on to contrast the relatively well-qualified workforce with the relatively poor performance of the economy, a contrast that would motivate and define the development of a skills strategy.

In response to this analysis of Scotland's economic performance, and in pursuit of its declared political objective of independence for Scotland, the Government set a single purpose of creating 'a more successful country with opportunities for all of Scotland to flourish, through sustainable economic growth' (Scottish Government, 2007a: 1). This is still a twin-track goal but with a clear priority focus on economic growth, which was to be achieved through raising labour productivity, increasing the rate of participation in the economy and increasing the population, by reducing outward migration and increasing inward migration. Some of the rhetoric of a global knowledge economy and the related importance of human capital is retained, but there is little mention of increasing the skills in the workforce and there are more references to maximising the value of the existing skills base.

Scottish Government skills policy from 2007

Skills for Scotland (Scottish Government, 2007b), a new 'lifelong skills strategy', was published within the first three months of the new administration. It is designed to be distinctively Scottish and to contrast with the Leitch Review of Skills (Leitch, 2006) (which covered the whole of the UK). This illustrates the potential for tension between a nationalist government in Scotland and a pro-unionist Westminster government. The Leitch Review of Skills is underpinned by an assumption that skills supply is the main problem and that issues of skills demand and usage will ultimately take care of themselves (Keep, 2008a, 2009). Felstead (2007) suggested that, on the contrary, improvements in the supply of qualified individuals had outstripped the needs of the Scottish economy due, in part, to the profile of jobs within the labour market. These research findings suggested that issues of demand and utilisation are more important enablers of improved economic performance than boosting the percentage of qualified workers. *Skills for Scotland* cites other similar research evidence about the operation of the labour market (for example Autor *et al.*, 2002; Felstead *et al.*, 2007). Based on this body of evidence, *Skills for Scotland* accepts that simply adding more skills to the workforce will not secure the full benefit for the economy unless employers and individuals change their behaviour to become 'ambitious and demanding users of skills' (p. 13). Furthermore, there is a recognition that skills interact in clear, if complex, ways with other drivers of productivity such as capital investment and innovation. The main theme of the strategy is to capitalise on what Scotland has by way of its population and its learning system and to make it work better through boosting demand (from both employers and individuals) rather than expanding the supply side. In summary, *Skills for Scotland* sets out an intention to improve the supply of skills; to drive up demand from individuals and employers; and to improve the usage of skills in the workplace.

This policy therefore marks a departure both from the Westminster Government direction set by Leitch and from the previous policy stance in Scotland, in a number of ways. *Skills for Scotland* is a 'cradle to grave' strategy, which recombines policy for education, skills and lifelong learning and therefore presages a broader span of interventions across a continuum of provision. It seeks to balance the needs of employers and individuals. It offers an inclusive approach to policy development and delivery, with distinct and ambitious roles for all stakeholders within a more joined-up learning system. There is no commitment to greater levels of investment in 'stockpiling' intermediate qualifications. We argue that this is not a deficit model that identifies problems requiring government-led fixes. By contrast this purports to be a model that builds on strengths and requires all stakeholders to do better with existing resources. The strategy was generally well received by business and by commentators, who welcomed the prospect of informed debate about skills utilisation and complimented the Scottish Government for taking a lead on integrating skills policy within a wider business improvement, innovation and economic development agenda (Keep, 2008b).

At the time of writing it is too early to attempt an evaluation of this new strategic direction for skills and lifelong learning policy because it has been in place for less then three years. We will, however, critically review here the innovative directions signalled in the policy. We will focus on how they have been converted into a programme of strategic change and we will consider the barriers to progress.

Scotland's focus on skills utilisation

Perhaps the most distinctive feature of *Skills for Scotland* is its focus on improving the utilisation of skills in the workplace. 'Skills utilisation' has become a pervasive feature of discourse on skills in Scotland, through the activity of the Skills Utilisation Leadership Group, which is chaired by the Cabinet Secretary for Education and Lifelong Learning and whose role is 'to champion the effective use of skills in the workplace' (see <www.scotland. gov.uk/Topics/Education/skills-strategy/making-skills-work/utilisation/

SkillsUtilisation>). This Group has provided a locus for a very busy agenda of research, publications, debate and awareness-raising activity, which has been documented on a comprehensive website (Scottish Government, 2010a). We believe that some consideration of how the Government has set about influencing practice within the workplace, given that capitalising on the existing skills of the workforce requires different behaviours on the part of employers and employees, is appropriate. Influencing the supply of vocational training is relatively easy for governments to do and it has therefore tended to be the policy lever of choice for this reason (Field, 2000). Improving and increasing demand for and deployment of skills is more difficult.

One step that governments can take is to improve the responsiveness of the education and training system so that employers find it easy to source, and therefore demand, relevant skills training (Ashton, 2006; Sung et al., 2006). In England there is evidence of this approach in the enhanced role given to Sector Skills Councils (SSCs) to articulate employer demand and, to some extent, to determine what courses and curriculum should be approved (UKCES, 2009). The use of financial incentives such as the Train to Gain initiative (BIS, 2010) in England (see note at the end of Chapter 2 for more information on this initiative) are also clearly aimed at bringing employer demand to bear on training providers by routing some funding through employers and employer-led bodies.

In Scotland, a different approach can be observed. *Skills for Scotland* gives SSCs a broader advisory role rather than a controlling one and directs them primarily to deliver high-quality labour market information that will influence learning at all levels, and not just specific vocational qualifications. Financial incentives to persuade employers to undertake more training are rejected because they are unlikely to be effective and they risk displacing money that employers would have spent anyway. Instead there is a softer approach, to support the capacity of learning providers to understand and respond to employer needs. Here we see evidence of the positive relationship in Scotland between the government and learning providers, particularly colleges, as described earlier. Colleges are viewed as respected partners that can be trusted to respond to government priorities rather than manipulated into doing so by financial levers and contractual relationships. The Scottish Funding Council (SFC) has taken some steps to put into practice this softer approach to improving the responsiveness of colleges to employer demand, by allocating funds for employer engagement and knowledge exchange, and by funding a programme of 'skills utilisation' action research projects, primarily designed to build better working relationships between universities, colleges and employers (SFC, 2009a). The SFC has also commissioned a programme of projects in work-related learning, work placements, enterprise and workforce development to improve the relevance of curricula to the workplace (SFC, 2009b).

Important though a responsive education and training system is, it is unlikely on its own to deliver higher levels of skills and a corresponding beneficial effect on employer ambition and performance. If employers are to be encouraged to develop more ambitious business strategies requiring higher skill levels, government has to find new policy levers or apply available levers in new ways. The Skills Utilisation Leadership Group's commissioned literature survey identified a typology of interventions in evidence in other countries, particularly Australia, New Zealand and Finland, defined as holistic or 'eco-system' strategies, market-led workplace strategies (such as High Performance Working on which there is an extensive literature) and government-led workplace strategies (CFE, 2008). Despite its apparent interest in these international comparators, the Scottish Government has to date shown no indication of willingness to commit resources to a programme of direct intervention in skills utilisation either at the workplace level or through sectoral eco-system projects.

Sung *et al.* (2009), in research undertaken in Scotland, sought to understand the factors that shape employers' product market strategies and the specific role that public policy can play, especially in influencing how firms utilise skills in their competitive strategies, recognising that skills should be a derived demand. This study suggests that, although changes in market conditions are the major factor in influencing change in firms' competitive strategies, public policy can play a part. Available policy levers might include, on the one hand, regulatory and legislative standards, and the development of criteria for compliance for awards or grading systems; and, on the other hand, collaborative 'branding initiatives'. In certain circumstances direct action through, for example, conditions of grant and procurement can also be effective. The analysis concludes that sectoral differentiation is essential and that there is no 'silver bullet'. These conclusions are echoed in the findings of a commissioned investigation into best practices in selected workplaces, which concluded that there was no common factor in evidence, but that culture and values and product/market forces were the strongest determinants of positive skills formation and utilisation practice (SQW Consulting, 2010).

It is perhaps worth considering what employers themselves have to say about driving up economic performance through usage of skills. Discussion in the National Economic Forum advocated government leadership, the encouragement of good practice, improved dialogue between industry and learning providers and preparing individuals better for the workplace (Scottish Government, 2010b). On the basis of this agenda, set by business leaders themselves, and of the research evidence noted above, there is some cause for optimism. There is currently no evidence of intention to use the policy levers identified by Sung *et al.* (2009). The Government has, however, through the Skills Utilisation Leadership Group and its associated cross-sectoral network, communication strategy and employer engagement strategy, set out to bring about the changes advocated by business leaders, through leading a pervasive and persuasive dialogue (Scottish Government, 2010a). This is an approach that may prove to be feasible in a country the size of Scotland.

A different landscape in Scotland

The SNP Government has resisted the temptation to create or reform funding and delivery agencies for post-school learning, in marked contrast to England (Munro, 2010). Only one new agency, Skills Development Scotland (SDS), has been created, to bring together information, advice and guidance services (previously provided by Careers Scotland as part of Scottish Enterprise (SE) and Highlands and Islands Enterprise (HIE) and by LearnDirect Scotland) with the administration of national training programmes (also previously undertaken by SE and HIE). The intention is to create a strategic skills body that will transform skills performance in Scotland. This is an ambitious goal for a new agency with a relatively modest budget of £200 million per annum. SDS's brief to improve advice and guidance services for individuals creates tension at the point of interface between devolved skills policy and non-devolved employment and social security policy, and this may prove to be politically important for a nationalist government. With the exception of the creation of SDS, the Government's approach has been to demand that existing agencies both operate more cohesively and contribute more demonstrably to the Government's national performance framework of purpose, targets, objectives, outcomes and indicators (Scottish Government, 2007c). There are many instances of more collaborative practice in policy implementation within the public sector generally and in the skills and lifelong learning sector in particular, one example being a joint Skills Committee between the SFC and SDS.

Skills for Scotland also placed importance on building individual demand for learning and here there is less evidence of clear direction. Scotland has not embarked on any radical reform of post-16 qualifications that might extend the choices available to individuals, for example through work-based or vocational routes to higher education. The provision of Higher National Certificate (HNC) and Higher National Diploma (HND) courses in Scotland's colleges has contributed to increased participation rates in higher education in Scotland (Lowe, 2005; Gallacher, 2009a), but a recent HN modernisation programme went no further than updating the curricula. Foundation Degrees have not been adopted (Gallacher *et al.*, 2009). The abolition of tuition fees for higher education, whilst undoubtedly popular, has not only created potential challenges for funding higher education, but has exacerbated inequities in funding regimes for full-time and part-time students. *Skills for Scotland* acknowledges that individuals and employers should make decisions based on the learning that is most useful to them and not on the availability of financial support, and the reintroduction of Individual Learning Accounts offers some redress for those wishing to study part-time (Gallacher, 2009b). *Skills for Scotland*, however, is silent on how a more coherent and equitable system of determining who pays for what in post-school education might be achieved.

2010: Response to recession

Skills for Scotland attempted to set a distinctive policy direction for Scotland in post-school education and training, and there is some evidence of progress towards a more cohesive system, and in developing and communicating a pervasive and persuasive discourse about 'skills utilisation'. Improving skills utilisation is not amenable to short-term interventions and it remains to be seen whether this policy direction will be maintained into the longer term, and whether ways can be found of appropriately measuring policy effects. Recent developments suggest that the imperative of acting to ameliorate the effects of the economic recession may have caused the Government to revert to more traditional policies of increasing participation through expansion of the supply of learning opportunities, as a way of combating unemployment. Certainly there has been increased investment in vocational training, particularly Modern Apprenticeships, through new financial incentives to employers. This carries the risk of reinforcing employer perceptions that the government pays for skills training. Priority for expansion of places in colleges has been accorded to areas of highest unemployment and social deprivation. It is perhaps disappointing that these increases in the volume of education and training have not, as yet, been subject to any test of their relevance to the jobs that might be available post-recession.

An updated version of *Skills for Scotland,* entitled *Skills for Scotland: Accelerating the recovery and increasing sustainable economic growth* (Scottish Government, 2010c), was published in October 2010, in a different political and economic context from that of the original document. Politically, it represents an opportunity for the SNP Government to oppose the programme of drastic reductions in public expenditure that has been initiated by the UK Coalition Government. For this reason, and in response to the effects of the economic downturn in Scotland, the revised skills strategy reverts to presenting increased access to learning provision as a solution to current problems of redundancies and unemployment and then cataloguing government investments and tactical interventions. The case for driving up demand for, and utilisation of, skills as part of an overarching purpose of sustainable economic growth has not been abandoned, and indeed remains a clearly stated element of the revised strategy. The imperative to deal with the recession and to prepare for the 2011 election in Scotland inevitably means that debate about the relative priority of investment in the supply of learning will return to centre stage.

Conclusion

This chapter has presented an overview of post-16 education and training policy in Scotland post-devolution, as expressed in policy statements and government-led policy initiatives, and has documented evidence of both continuity and change within Scotland. Policy statements are, however, only one component of political and social change. The implementation of policy and its eventual relevance for citizens is the result of a more complex set of economic, social and professional processes. The interplay between governments at all levels, agencies, institutions and individuals takes place over a longer timescale than policy papers suggest. We conclude that whether or not post-devolution governments in Scotland deliver a continuing evolution of Scotland's already distinctive education system, or whether they achieve and sustain a more radical change of direction, remains a matter for future empirical analyses.

Notes

1   Learndirect Scotland was the brand name for the University for Industry in Scotland. It established a national learning opportunities database, a contact centre and a network of branded learning centres. Its functions were transferred to Skills Development Scotland (SDS) in 2008.

2   Future Skills Scotland was established as part of Scottish Enterprise. Its functions were transferred into the Scottish Government in 2010.

3   Careers Scotland was Scotland's careers service for school pupils originally offered by local authorities. The first Scottish Government transferred it to SE and Highlands and Islands Enterprise (HIE) as a new all age service. It was then transferred to SDS in 2008.

4   For details, see <www.scqf.org.uk>.

5   For example, the proportion of employers providing training declined between 2003 and 2004; enrolments in further education declined in 2003–04 and 2004–05; numbers starting a Modern Apprenticeship declined in 2005–06.

6   SCQF Level 9 is the equivalent of an ordinary degree.

References

Ashton, D. (2006) 'Lessons from abroad: Developing sector based approaches to skills'. *Catalyst*, Issue 2. Wath-upon-Dearne: Sector Skills Development Agency.

Autor, D., Levy, F. and Murnane, R. (2002) 'Upstairs, downstairs: Computers and skills on two floors of a large bank'. *Industrial and Labour Relations Review*, 55(3), 432–47.

Byrne, D. and Raffe, D. (2005) *Establishing a UK 'Home International' Comparative Research Programme for Post-Compulsory Learning*. London: Learning and Skills Development Agency.

CFE (2008) *Skills Utilisation Literature Review*. Edinburgh: Scottish Government <http://www.scotland.gov.uk/Publications/2008/12/15114643/16> (accessed 12 April 2010).

Coffield, F. (1997) 'Introduction and overview: Attempts to reclaim the concept of the learning society'. *Journal of Education Policy*, 12(6), 449–55.

Cubie, A. (1999) *Student Finance: Fairness for the future*. Edinburgh: HMSO.

Department for Business, Innovation and Skills (BIS) (2010) *Train to Gain*. <http://www.bis.gov.uk/assets/biscore/corporate/docs/t/train-to-gain-feb-2009.pdf> (accessed 17 April 2010).

Department for Education and Employment (DfEE) (1998) *The Learning Age: Renaissance for a new Britain*. London: HMSO.

Felstead, A. (2007) *How 'Smart' are Scottish jobs? Summary evidence from the Skills Surveys, 1997–2006*. Glasgow: Scottish Enterprise.

Felstead, A., Gallie, G., Green, F. and Zhou, Y. (2007) *Skills at Work 1986–2006*. Oxford/Cardiff: SKOPE.

Field, J. (2000) *Lifelong Learning and the New Social Order*. Stoke-on-Trent: Trentham.

Fryer, R.H. (1997) *Learning for the Twenty-First Century: First report of the National Advisory Group on Continuing Education and Lifelong Learning*. London: DfEE.

Gallacher, J. (2009a) 'Higher education in Scotland's colleges: A distinctive tradition?'. *Higher Education Quarterly*, 63(4), 304–401.

Gallacher, J. (2009b) *Inquiry into the Future of Lifelong Learning: The Scottish Perspective*. <http://www.niace.org.uk/lifelonglearninginquiry/default.htm> (accessed 28 April 2010).

Gallacher, J., Ingram, R. and Reeve, F. (2009) *Work Based and Work Related Learning in Higher National Certificates and Diplomas in Scotland and Foundation*

Degrees in England: A comparative study. Glasgow: Centre for Research in Lifelong Learning, Glasgow Caledonian University.

Keep, E. (2008a) *A Comparison of the Welsh Assembly Government's Workforce Development Programme and England's Train to Gain*. SKOPE Research Paper No. 79. Cardiff: Cardiff University.

-- (2008b) 'The big skills fix'. *Herald Scotland*, 15 March 2008. <http://www.heraldscotland.com/the-big-skills-fix-1.834140> (accessed 12 April 2010).

-- (2009) *The Limits of the Possible: Shaping the learning and skills landscape through a shared policy narrative*. SKOPE Research Paper No. 8. Cardiff: Cardiff University.

Kennedy, H. (1997) *Learning Works*. Coventry: Further Education Funding Council.

Leitch, S. (2005) *Skills in the UK: The long-term challenge*. Interim Report. London: HM Treasury.

-- (2006) *Prosperity for All in the Global Economy: World class skills*. Final Report. London: HM Treasury.

Lowe, J. (2005) *Integrating Learning with Life: A study of higher education students in a Scottish further education college: 2000–2003*. Unpublished Ed.D. thesis. <http://dspace.stir.ac.uk/dspace/handle/1893/66> (accessed 11 April 2006).

McTavish, D. (2003) 'Aspects of public sector management: A case study of further education, 10 years from the passage of the Further and Higher Education Act'. *Educational Management and Administration*, 31(2), 175–85.

Munro, N. (2010) 'Radical overhaul sees FE in England veer away from Scottish system'. *Times Educational Supplement*, Scotland, 9 April, p. 18.

Rees, G. (2002) 'Devolution and re-structuring post-16 education and training in the UK'. In J. Adams and P. Robinson (eds), *Devolution in Practice: Public policy differences within the UK*. London: Institute for Public Policy Research.

Scottish Executive (1999) *Making It Work Together*. Edinburgh: The Stationery Office.

-- (2001a) *Working Together for Scotland*. Edinburgh: The Stationery Office.

-- (2001b) *Further Education in Scotland 2000*. <http://.scotland.gov.uk/Resource/Doc/158956/0043193.pdf> (accessed 27 July 2009).

-- (2003a) *A Framework for Higher Education in Scotland*. Edinburgh: The Stationery Office.

-- (2003b) *Life Through Learning Through Life*. Edinburgh: The Stationery Office.

-- (2004) *The Competitiveness of Higher Education in Scotland: Higher Education Review*. Edinburgh: The Stationery Office.

-- (2004) *A Smart, Successful Scotland: Strategic direction to the Enterprise Networks and an enterprise strategy for Scotland*. Edinburgh: The Stationery Office.

-- (2006) *Strategy Update*. Edinburgh: The Stationery Office.

Scottish Funding Council (SFC) (2009a) *Skills Utilisation Projects: Progress report*. <http://www.sfc.ac.uk/about_the_council/council_board_committees/ Committeepapers/2009/SkillsCommittee26November2009.aspx> (accessed 17 April 2010).

-- (2009b) *Learning to Work Two: Developing the Council's employability strategy*. <http://www.sfc.ac.uk/news_events_circulars/Circulars/2009/ SFC4109.aspx> (accessed 17 April 2010).

Scottish Government (2007a) *The Government Economic Strategy*. Edinburgh: The Scottish Government.

-- (2007b) *Skills for Scotland*. Edinburgh: The Scottish Government.

-- (2007c) Scottish Budget Spending Review. <http://www.scotland.gov.uk/ Publications/2007/11/13092240/9> (accessed 17 April 2010).

-- (2010a) *Skills Utilisation Leadership Group*. <http://www.scotland.gov. uk/Topics/Education/skills-strategy/making-skills-work/utilisation/ SkillsUtilisation> (accessed 12 April 2010).

-- (2010b) *National Economic Forum Key Messages*. <http://www.scotland.gov. uk/Resource/Doc/980/0076458.doc> (accessed 12 April 2010).

-- (2010c) *Skills for Scotland: Accelerating the recovery and increasing sustainable economic growth*. Edinburgh: The Scottish Government. <http://www.scotland. gov.uk/Publications/2010/10/04125111/0> (accessed 19 October 2010).

Scottish Office (1998) *Opportunity Scotland*. Edinburgh: The Stationery Office.

Scottish Parliament Enterprise and Culture Committee (2003) *Scottish Solutions*. Norwich: The Stationery Office.

Scottish Parliament Enterprise and Lifelong Learning Committee (2002) *Report on Lifelong Learning*. Norwich: The Stationery Office.

SQW Consulting (2010) *Best Strategies in Skills Utilisation*. <http://www.scottish-enterprise.com/about-us/research-publications/~/media/publications/ About%20Us/economic%20research/skills-utilisation-report-final.ashx> (accessed 19 October 2010).

Sung, J., Ashton, D. and Raddon, A. (2009) *Product Market Strategies and Workforce Skills.* Future Skills Scotland. <http://www.scotland.gov.uk/Resource/Doc/276658/0083070.pdf> (accessed 12 April 2010).

Sung, J., Raddon, A. and Ashton, D. (2006) *Skills Abroad: A comparative assessment of international policy approaches to skills leading to the development of policy recommendations for the UK.* SSDA Research Report 16. Wath-upon-Dearne: Sector Skills Development Agency.

Tight, M. (1998) 'Lifelong learning: Opportunity or compulsion?'. *British Journal of Educational Studies*, 46(3), 251–63.

United Kingdom Commission for Education and Skills (UKCES) (2009) *Five-Year Strategic Plan 2009–2014*. London: UKCES.

Chapter 4

Devolution, policy-making and lifelong learning: The case of Wales

Gareth Rees

Introduction: The changing context

The results of the General Election of May 2010 serve to underline the enduring political differences between the constituent territories of the United Kingdom. Once again we are reminded that the Conservatives are essentially an English party in their capacity to win seats (notwithstanding their modest advances in Wales). In both Wales and Scotland, the political landscape continues to reflect a broadly social democratic consensus, albeit with significant nationalist inflections.[1] Therefore, the established Scottish National Party minority Scottish government and the Labour–Plaid Cymru coalition administration in Wales will have to engage with the new Conservative–Liberal Democrat coalition at the UK level. At the time of writing, however, it remains to be seen exactly what impacts this change in the political complexion of the UK Government will have on its relationships with the devolved administrations in Cardiff and Edinburgh.

Nevertheless, even at this stage, it is clear that developing these new relationships will be made more difficult by the testing economic conditions that will prevail for – at least – the medium term. More specifically, key areas of contention will be the intensely ideological issues of the appropriate nature of the public sector and, crucially, the scope of the expenditure necessary to sustain it. Moreover, as the new Conservative–Liberal Democrat Coalition Government begins to announce its initial policy programme, it is increasingly clear that its impacts on the different parts of the UK will be sharply differentiated. Most significantly, the effects of cuts in public expenditure will be felt most sharply in those areas where the public sector accounts for a much larger part of economic activity. In Wales, for example, the proportion of employment accounted for by the public sector is significantly higher than that for the UK as a whole; in 2007, the figures were some 24 per cent in Wales compared with just under 20 per cent for the UK as a whole (Statistics for Wales, 2009); and the vulnerability of Wales in current conditions is thus intensified.

These changing circumstances pose very sharp questions as to the extent to which the system of parliamentary devolution initiated in 1999 can produce significant differences in policies and patterns of expenditure between the constituent countries of the UK. Simply put, how far can the devolved administrations pursue policies that, in effect, insulate Scotland and Wales from the effects of the policies being implemented by the UK Government? Of course, in general terms, this is not a new question. The extent to which the devolved administrations have been able to instigate policies that are distinctive to their own priorities, reflecting what are seen to be the specificities of their national economic and social needs, has been explored almost since the inception of the devolved constitutional system over a decade ago (e.g. Adams and Robinson, 2002). Nevertheless, such questions are likely to be posed especially acutely in the inevitably difficult circumstances of the coming years.

It is worth emphasising here that these questions need to be posed about the Welsh situation, just as much as about that in Scotland. The fact that the constitutional settlement devolved significantly more powers to the Scottish Parliament than to the National Assembly for Wales has perhaps diverted attention from the extent to which, nevertheless, Wales has been enabled to pursue a distinctive policy agenda. Moreover, since the 2006 Government of Wales Act, the National Assembly has been empowered to enact legislation for Wales, known as 'Assembly Measures' (the equivalent of Parliamentary Acts), in the fields over which it has legislative competence (although the designation of new fields is subject to a complex process of scrutiny by the UK Government and the Westminster Parliament).

Certainly, education and training is a field in which, both before and after the 2006 Act, a distinctive policy agenda has been developed in Wales. The Welsh Assembly Government (WAG) has pursued its own priorities, building on the national educational strategy set out in 2001 (National Assembly for Wales, 2001). Only some aspects of this distinctive system – such as the abolition of Key Stage testing and associated 'league tables'[2] – have been widely remarked outside of Wales. However, in reality, it is reflected across all the phases of education, from the Foundation Phase provision for early years, to a commitment to non-selective, 'community-based' comprehensive schools at the secondary level, new curriculum provision for 14–19 year olds through the Learning Pathways and the Welsh Baccalaureate, and, most recently, innovative provision for the organisation and funding of higher education (Rees, 2002, 2004, 2007; Rees and Taylor, 2006). For the purposes of this chapter, it is especially instructive that one of the early Assembly Measures was the 2009 Learning and Skills (Wales) Measure, which – *inter alia* – created a statutory basis for a minimum curriculum provision in local areas for 14–19 year olds. As this minimum includes both academic and vocational options, this, in turn, necessitates the development of new forms of collaboration between secondary schools, further education colleges and private training providers (an issue that is discussed in greater detail later in this chapter).

There are ample grounds, therefore, for arguing that parliamentary devolution has created the space for the development of distinctive Welsh policies for education and training. It is much more complex, of course, to demonstrate the effects of this policy system on educational outcomes such as access to educational opportunities, patterns of participation or attainment levels, let alone the educational experiences of pupils and students in a wider sense. Certainly, some commentators have suggested that the fact that attainment levels (as reflected in Key Stage scores, GCSE performance and PISA results) in Wales are broadly worse than those in England is attributable to the shortcomings of the Welsh education system, both in terms of its policies and levels of funding (Reynolds, 2008). However, more sophisticated empirical work than has been carried out so far would be required to establish a robust foundation for this contention. Indeed, it is arguable that many of the policies have been introduced too recently for any well-founded analysis of their effects to be carried out as yet. This is certainly the case if one looks beyond the performance of the educational system itself to consider the impacts of educational change on wider outcomes, such as economic growth or social mobility.

For the moment, therefore, there are good, pragmatic grounds for focusing on the nature of the policies themselves and the processes through which they have come about; and it is these issues that constitute the principal concerns of this chapter. More specifically, the focus is on the development of policies aimed at restructuring the post-16 provision of education and training, after the compulsory phase has been completed (although higher education is largely excluded from the discussion). The aim, however, is not to provide an exhaustive account of the policies themselves; but rather to explore how the devolved policy system in Wales has worked to produce its distinctive approach to these issues. Addressing policy processes in this way provides one kind of analytical basis for approaching the questions raised earlier in this chapter about the likely impacts of the economic and political changes that Wales – as elsewhere – is currently experiencing. An improved understanding of how Welsh policies for post-16 learning and skills have come about hitherto provides an indication of the scope of what the 1999 devolution settlement has made possible and, thereby, the limits and possibilities of future developments in what will be very different circumstances.

Ideology matters: Lifelong learning and the social democratic consensus

One of the effects of the devolution settlement of 1999 has been to intensify the impact of a distinctively Welsh politics on the development of policies in Wales. In ways that were clearly intended by its architects, parliamentary devolution has created the circumstances in which, at least in those policy fields where powers are devolved, policies can be developed that, to a much greater extent than hitherto, reflect the political priorities represented through the National Assembly and the WAG. This, in turn, implies that it is difficult to understand the form of Welsh policies without reference to the wider ideological context within which these political priorities are shaped.

Mention has already been made of the broad social democratic consensus which characterises the Welsh political landscape. In part, this simply reflects the key role that the Labour Party continues to play in all aspects of Welsh political life. Certainly, Labour has been by far the largest party in the National Assembly since its creation in 1999, although it has not been able to secure significant majorities over all the other parties combined.[3] This has resulted in its leading coalition administrations for much of this period, with the Liberal Democrats between 2000 and 2003, and since 2007 with Plaid Cymru. These coalitions have been based on agreed policy programmes. The current Labour–Plaid Cymru coalition, for example, is founded on an explicit agreement, negotiated during the protracted aftermath of the 2007 Assembly Election and summarised in the *One Wales* document, setting out the principal dimensions of a four-year policy programme (WAG, 2007).

However, it is important to understand that, in ideological terms, Labour in Wales has remained distinct from New Labour (Paterson, 2003). Indeed, in a much-quoted speech in 2002, the then First Minister, Rhodri Morgan, was at pains to draw attention to the 'clear red water' between the approach to the provision of public services being adopted in Wales and that of New Labour in England (Morgan, 2002). What was involved here was more than simply the rejection of New Labour's policies that preoccupied the London-based media for a short time. It also reflected a positive commitment to forms of public service provision that embody alternative ideological priorities that are seen to be specifically attuned to Welsh needs (Drakeford, 2005). Moreover, this commitment extends beyond the Labour Party in Wales to include the Liberal Democrats and Plaid Cymru, as is reflected in the largely smooth-running coalition administrations. Even elements of the Welsh Conservatives have come to accept some of these priorities, albeit in somewhat attenuated forms.

Certainly, in the field of education, it is clear that the rationale for pursuing a 'Welsh route' has been as much about ideology as efficiency; it expresses profoundly held beliefs about how the education system and the learning opportunities it provides *ought* to be organised in Wales. The specific commitment here has been to what may be seen as deep-seated, social democratic virtues, tailored to changed circumstances. For example, there has been an emphasis on the rights and obligations of citizenship, expressed most clearly through the notion of the 'entitlements' of children and young people (most recently drawing on the United Nations Convention on the Rights of the Child). Educational provision, in which the state's role is seen to be essential, aims at ensuring equality of opportunity through universal provision. Citizen 'voice' (of students, parents, professionals and community groups) is preferred to marketised forms of consumer 'choice' as a means of developing educational provision. Partnership and collaboration between the central state, local education authorities and professional groups are seen as the most effective means of developing and implementing educational policy; and so on (Rees, 2007).

These essentially ideological principles, in turn, have provided a framework within which specific policies have been created. This does not imply, of course, that specific policies are somehow *entailed* by political priorities; policies cannot simply be 'read off' from the ideological priorities. Rather, there is a powerful set of shared assumptions about the general approach that should be adopted; and, by implication at least, the sorts of approaches which do not accord with the 'Welsh way of doing things'.

This is clearly illustrated in the distinctive approach that has been adopted by the WAG to curriculum provision for 14–19 year olds through its Learning Pathways programme. Hence, the emphasis upon citizen entitlement provides the ideological foundation for the requirement – given *statutory* authority in the 2009 Learning and Skills (Wales) Measure – that every 14 year old will (by 2012) be able to choose from a minimum of 30 course options, rising to 40 options for post-16 provision (although this latter is not yet a statutory requirement). Moreover, the notion of entitlement extends to the *form* of learning opportunities that are to be available. Accordingly, the Learning and Skills Measure also stipulates that there will have to be a minimum number of vocational courses available to learners of all abilities, as well as the academic options. A recent Estyn study (2010) indicates that there has already been substantial progress towards achieving these curriculum requirements, with most schools already meeting the minimum requirements of the Measure for 2012. The significant widening of choices available to learners – especially with respect to vocational options – is reported to be having positive impacts on attendance, behaviour and attainment.[4] Improving provision in this way, in turn, is seen to provide the basis for enhancing levels of participation post-16, without introducing the requirement to do so (as has been introduced in England, through the raising of the statutory minimum age for leaving education and training).

In addition, since 2003, there has been a progressive extension of the scope of the Welsh Baccalaureate Qualification (the 'Welsh Bacc'), at

Foundation, Intermediate and Advanced levels. The Welsh Bacc offers a single, umbrella qualification, within which students can incorporate options, such as GCSEs, AS and A Levels, as well as BTECs, NVQs and the Principal Learning and Project elements of the English 14–19 Diplomas (which have not otherwise been adopted in Wales). In addition, students are required to complete a Core, comprising key skills, and work-related and personal and social education, along with modules on 'Wales, Europe and the World' and an individual investigation. It is intended that the Welsh Bacc should become available to all learners in Wales in due course. It is clearly possible that it will eventually provide a framework for moving beyond the current optional qualifications and instituting a wholly distinctive curriculum, characterised by much more porous boundaries between academic and vocational programmes. This was certainly the vision elaborated in the Webb Review, a major analysis of further education in Wales commissioned by the WAG (Webb Review, 2007). It has to be acknowledged, however, that realising this vision will require considerable further development.

Not surprisingly, delivering this curriculum entitlement has necessitated a very significant restructuring of the system of provision. Most striking about what has been termed the 'transformation' policy is that it reflects very clearly the ideological commitment to partnership and collaboration that is integral to the Welsh approach to public services provision. As elaborated initially in a WAG strategy document, *Skills that Work for Wales* (DCELLS, 2008a), local authorities and post-16 education and training providers were required to produce proposals for Learning Partnerships in local areas that could *demonstrate* their capacity to deliver the new curriculum requirements (and, indeed, provision for all post-16 learners) in an effective and efficient way. The precise number and form of the Learning Partnerships were left to be determined at the local level, although the WAG did set out a number of possible, alternative models (DCELLS, 2008b). Perhaps most significantly, where proposals for Learning Partnerships have been deemed to be unsatisfactory, the WAG has adopted what it terms 'a more interventionist approach' with some alacrity; and has insisted on an implementation schedule whereby 60 per cent of changes overall should be in the implementation phase by September 2010 and the remainder by the following year (DCELLS, 2009).[5]

By July 2009, almost 30 transformation proposals had been received by the WAG. Fourteen of these involve establishing systematic collaboration between schools and further education colleges, using new WAG regulations to permit the creation of formal governance and management arrangements across a local area. In five areas, proposals involve the creation of tertiary systems for the delivery of post-16 provision, often including elements of higher education delivery too and linking with wider strategies for economic regeneration of severely disadvantaged areas.[6] There are six mergers between further education colleges underway, two of which have already taken place.

In two rural areas, wholesale reorganisation of the education and training system is proposed, from early years provision onwards (DCELLS, 2009). However, as the recent Estyn study (2010) makes clear, it remains the case that progress towards the effective *implementation* of these proposals remains uneven across the different local authority areas.

Clearly, in developing these proposals, pragmatic considerations have played a part. Certainly, the Webb Review (2007) drew attention to the significance of the practical implications of demographic change in the proliferation of under-sized school sixth forms and the small size and low turnover of many further education colleges. Institutional collaboration through the Learning Partnerships provides a means of addressing these problems, albeit complicated by the particular problems associated with provision for sparsely populated, rural areas and for appropriate levels of Welsh-medium and bilingual programmes. Nevertheless, it remains the case that the commitment to the virtue of collaborative approaches to service provision constitutes a powerful framing of appropriate policies too.

More generally as well, the effects of the ideological priorities that underpin Welsh politics on policies for post-16 education and training are real enough. There is a distinctive 'policy repertoire' in Wales that reflects these priorities and that provides at least part of the explanation of how actual policies have taken the form that they have. Parliamentary devolution has established the mechanisms through which Wales can pursue this distinctive policy agenda, thereby creating the potential for divergence with the other countries of the UK (and with England, in particular).

Lifelong learning and the Welsh policy community

The impacts of the social democratic consensus in Wales are, of course, expressed within processes of policy-making, which extend beyond the WAG and the National Assembly. There is a wider system of governance that embraces not only the different elements of the central state (government ministers, their advisors, civil servants, Assembly Members and so on), but also the various 'arm's length' agencies (formally, Assembly Government Sponsored Bodies) and the local authorities. It also encompasses bodies that represent different interests within civil society (employers' organisations, trade unions, voluntary associations, think tanks and so forth) and which seek to influence the formation of policy. It is the interactions within these wider policy networks through which broad ideological priorities get translated into actual initiatives within specific policy fields (Day *et al.*, 2006).[7] Certainly, in the field of education and training, it is difficult to understand the genesis and wider import of specific policies except by reference to the key roles of the local authorities or of agencies such as Estyn (the Welsh Inspectorate), as well as organisations representing key interest groups, such as the teacher trade unions (in schools, colleges and higher education) (Rees, 2007).

One of the key aspirations of the proponents of parliamentary devolution is to reconfigure Welsh policy networks in ways which not only make deliberations more transparent to the electorate, but also open up policy-making to much more inclusive forms of participation and influence. However, how far this aspiration has been achieved remains a matter that is disputed. Certainly, there are robust grounds for arguing that the post-1999 governance system has moved far beyond the very 'top-down' patterns of 'vertical partnership' that were characteristic of the Welsh Office's relationships with other agencies and organisations during the period of administrative devolution, prior to 1999 (Morgan et al., 1999).

Greater openness in the policy-making process is, at one level, a straightforward product of the basic architecture of the constitutional settlement itself. The National Assembly has 60 members through whom pressure can be exerted on the executive process. The Assembly Committees also provide much more open access for interest groups and individuals of all kinds to express their views in the process of policy development (Jones and Osmond, 2001). Moreover, at least during the early years of parliamentary devolution, the Committees exerted not inconsiderable influence on the WAG, as, for example, when the then Post-16 Education and Training Committee persuaded the Cabinet to limit the role of business interests in the learning and skills system, in favour of 'skills producers' in the local authorities and wider educational groupings (Morgan and Rees, 2001). More recently, however, and especially since the 2006 Government of Wales Act, the Committees have assumed what is essentially a scrutiny function, akin to the parliamentary committees at Westminster.

In addition, since 2006, a number of the principal Assembly Sponsored Public Bodies (as they were then known) have been absorbed into the WAG itself, becoming part of the civil service. These include key agencies within the field of education and training, such as the post-16 funding organisation, ELWa; the body responsible for the regulation of the curriculum, ACCAC; the Wales Youth Agency; the teacher continuing professional development body, Dysg; and most recently, Basic Skills Cymru. This 'bonfire of the quangos' had been a key element in the debates about the 'democratic deficit' in Wales prior to the 1997 devolution referendum, when it was justified in terms of increasing the democratic accountability of policy-making (Morgan and Mungham, 2000). Certainly, these changes imply that the Department for Children, Education, Lifelong Learning and Skills (DCELLS) in the WAG has a very powerful executive capacity, with responsibility for all aspects of policy development and implementation. It is also clear that the relationships of the politicians and civil servants within the Department with external interests and pressure groups are especially direct, having removed the buffer of the 'arm's length' agencies.

Nevertheless, there remains relatively little evidence to suggest that the new mechanisms for the formulation and development of education and training policy in Wales have – as yet at least – opened up avenues of influence to groupings in civil society that were previously excluded.[8] Rather, what appears to have happened is that the advent of parliamentary devolution has served to improve and intensify the interaction between those groups which have been central to the policy-making process all along. Certainly, for example, if one examines something as basic as the contributions to the formal public consultation exercises on its new education and training initiatives organised by the WAG, it is striking how far they are dominated by the local authorities (both individually and through the Welsh Local Government Association), professional bodies representing established educational interests (the teaching trade unions, for instance) and the regulatory bodies (such as Estyn).[9]

Some of the possibilities of this governance system and the policy networks it fosters can be illustrated by the response in Wales to the economic recession, which again emphasises the virtues of a collaborative approach. Since October 2008, the WAG has organised a series of Economic Summits (with the ninth being held in April 2010), which bring together the Government with representatives of employer organisations, the trade unions and the voluntary sector. The aim is to develop strategies to combat the effects of the recession, on the basis of mutual understanding of the issues and commitment to collaboration.[10]

This can be interpreted as a highly traditional response to economic difficulties, engaging very well established interests in the process of policy development. However, a number of initiatives have been developed that have attracted widespread interest for adopting a very different form of response to the recession from that being adopted elsewhere in the UK (and in England, in particular). Hence, for example, the ReACT scheme was extended significantly in October 2008 and provides training support for those who have recently been made redundant or who face the imminent possibility of being made so. By the end of 2009, some 12,000 individuals were participating in this programme; with 8 per cent of Jobseeker's Allowance claimants benefiting. Moreover, the ProAct initiative was created specifically to address the problems of the recession and provides funding to firms that are at risk of cutting jobs and/or moving to short-time working, with resources being made available for supporting wage costs and for employees to enhance their employability through training. By the end of 2009, almost 8,000 individuals were benefiting from this programme, with some 160 companies already involved and a further 130 in the pipeline (WAG, 2009).

In some ways, these distinctive initiatives grew out of the more general recognition among the education and training policy network in Wales that the approach adopted by the Leitch Review (Leitch, 2006) did not provide a satisfactory basis for the development of policy in Wales. Hence, Leitch's emphasis on the international benchmarking of stocks of qualifications and the need for further supply-side interventions to boost the levels of education and training taking place was quite quickly seen to offer relatively little to solving Welsh problems. As the highly influential Webb Review (2007) made clear, given the weakness of the Welsh economy, increasing the supply of skills through enhanced education and training would have to be matched by economic development strategies that increased levels of economic activity (especially in the most disadvantaged areas) and that, moreover, engaged directly with the ways in which employers make use of skills in the workplace. Certainly, Welsh strategy, as reflected in *Skills that Work for Wales* (DCELLS, 2008a), draws explicitly on this general analysis. Moreover, it has subsequently been taken up by the Wales Employment and Skills Board (WESB, 2010) which, along with its Scottish counterpart, has been influential in shaping the analysis presented by the UK Commission for Employment and Skills too (Keep *et al.*, 2010).

In this context, the approach adopted in the Workforce Development Programme, which has operated in Wales since 2005, is noteworthy. Here, a human resource development advisor on contract to WAG works with companies to improve their skills utilisation strategies and also facilitates access to the funding that would enable each company's learning plan to be implemented, on a matched funding basis. In this way, an attempt is made to link additional education and training directly to enhanced demand for skills within individual firms (Keep, 2008). It should be acknowledged, however, that the scope of the programme is relatively limited, although it has been expanded consistently since its inception and especially since the onset of the economic recession. During 2009, for example, almost 2,000 employers participated in the programme and received funding through it (WAG, 2009). It is also difficult to be categorical about the nature and extent of the impacts that the Programme has had on participating firms, although there is an abundance of highly supportive anecdotal evidence (see, for example, the Webb Review, 2007). Nevertheless, the Workforce Development Programme is important, if only as an indication of the potential for devising initiatives that set out to link skills supply with skills utilisation in an explicit and focused way.

In summary, then, the impacts of the governance system made possible by parliamentary devolution are complex. On the one hand, a distinctive and modestly imaginative set of policies for post-16 education and training has been developed, which appears to be tailored to the specificities of Welsh circumstances. On the other, the education and training policy network in Wales has not developed in ways that extend significantly the range of interests that are expressed within the policy-making process. Indeed, to some extent, the key arguments in the current debates about responses to the Leitch Review and the recession reflect deep-seated themes, which have preoccupied the policy network back to the 1990s and beyond. For example, many of the issues which preoccupied the Webb Review (2007) were the same as those which were the focus of the *Education and Training Action Plan for Wales* (Education and Training Action Group, 1999), which was published under the auspices of the Welsh Office, prior to the inception of parliamentary devolution (Morgan and Rees, 2001).

Lifelong learning, path dependency and the recession

In some regards, of course, it is asking a great deal of parliamentary devolution to produce a sea-change in the approaches adopted to the provision of post-16 education and training in Wales. Crucially here, the wider economic context within which this education and training is located has remained stubbornly unfavourable throughout the period since 1999 (despite the best efforts of the WAG and significant EU funding for the most disadvantaged areas). On all measures of economic activity, Wales has remained at a level very substantially below the UK average.[11] Hence, in 2008, Gross Value Added (GVA) per head in Wales was lower than in any other part of the UK. Wales also had the lowest average weekly earnings (in 2009) and the second-lowest household income (in 2008). Economic inactivity rates (in the first quarter of 2010) were higher than the other countries of the UK, except for Northern Ireland.

These general economic conditions are reflected in the demand for skills. For example, the Welsh economy is significantly less productive than any other part of the UK; if GVA per hour worked in the UK is set to 100, then in 2007, the Welsh figure was only 84.6. Moreover, Welsh GVA per hour worked fell by 9.5 per cent relative to the UK average between 1996 and 2007, the largest fall anywhere within the UK (UKCES, 2009). In addition, there are very few large, domestically owned and headquartered companies in Wales; and only a small financial sector. Public sector employment accounts for a relatively high proportion of the total (as discussed earlier). As a consequence, the demand for skills within Wales is significantly lower than in other parts of the UK, especially compared to areas such as London and the South East of England, where patterns of economic activity are so radically different (UKCES, 2009).

Not surprisingly, this low demand for skills is reflected in skills supply (insofar as this can be measured). Hence, Wales performs relatively badly in terms of the levels of qualifications held by working-age adults. In 2008, it had a higher proportion without any qualifications (almost 14 per cent) than either England or Scotland, although substantially lower than Northern Ireland. At the other end of the spectrum, its proportion of adults with higher-level qualifications (NQF Level 4 or above) was significantly lower than the other countries, except Northern Ireland. However, over the period between 1999 and 2008, the decrease in the proportion of adults with no qualifications was the largest; although this appears to be accounted for most substantially by the growth in numbers of individuals with relatively low qualification levels (up to NQF Level 2).

What this means, therefore, is that not only are there greater problems to be faced in Wales, but also the range of policy options is more restricted. Certainly, as the Webb Review (2007) recognised, it may be wholly appropriate to try to ensure that employers' views make a contribution to the development of curriculum and qualifications frameworks. However, given the present pattern of Welsh economic performance, it makes little sense to entrust the task of boosting skills levels simply to employers, who manifestly are not engaged in the sorts of production of goods and services that require high levels of skills currently. As the Wales Employment and Skills Board (2010) has argued, if improving skills levels is to be effective, 'there is a need to raise employer ambition – to encourage employers to raise their game and thereby demand more skills' (p. 25). However, what the experience of the past decade and more demonstrates is that shifting the established patterns of skills utilisation in Wales is especially intractable. It constitutes a clear exemplification of path dependency, where current problems reflect historical trajectories of development (Rees and Stroud, 2004).

It also needs to be borne in mind in this context that, despite the analysis presented earlier about the distinctiveness of Welsh policies for education and training, the scope of devolved policy-making is, in crucial aspects, restricted by the terms of the constitutional settlement itself. Especially in the current context of cuts in public expenditure, it is funding that will present the most pressing problems for post-16 education and training in Wales (as elsewhere in the UK and, indeed, more widely). For example, it is clear that the transformation policy discussed earlier is highly vulnerable to potential cuts in the capital expenditure programmes that underpin it (the Twenty-First Century Schools Programme, the Further Education Institution Investment Programme and the Higher Education Capital Expenditure Programme). More generally, recurrent expenditure in all areas is very unlikely to escape unscathed from the public expenditure cuts. Hence, for instance, although the WAG's funding of further education colleges in 2010–11 rose by 2.6 per cent, primarily as a result of the increased investment in adult skills during the economic recession, nine colleges have seen a reduction and all colleges are facing 'efficiency gains' of at least 5 per cent. The colleges have been warned to expect even tougher funding settlements in the three years 2011–12 to 2013–14, with possible annual cash reductions of 5 per cent. Moreover, a PricewaterhouseCoopers (2010) review of expenditure on education in Wales recently suggested that only 46 per cent of further education expenditure went on 'front-line' services of learning and teaching, which has been widely interpreted as presaging further cuts.

In this context, it is not surprising that the WAG and the National Assembly have become increasingly concerned about the Barnett Formula as the basis of financial allocations from the UK to the Welsh level of government, as is reflected most clearly in the deliberations of the Holtham Commission (ICFFW, 2009).[12] How far such deliberations will eventually lead to a funding system that reflects economic and social needs more accurately remains to be seen. However, in the meantime, the UK Government's somewhat improbable strategy is to resolve the general public expenditure problems before turning to any restructuring of the Barnett Formula. What this means, in turn, is that, for the foreseeable future, the direction, shape and levels of public policy interventions on post-16 education and training will continue to be constrained by the financial limitations built into the form that parliamentary devolution currently takes in Wales.

Acknowledgements

I am extremely grateful to Frank Coffield and my Cardiff colleagues, Sally Power, Chris Taylor and Richard Wyn Jones, for their insightful comments on an earlier version of this chapter.

Notes

1. Northern Ireland too continues to display a radically different politics from the remainder of the UK, albeit in ways that are distinctive from Scotland and Wales.

2. Key Stage assessment is retained, of course, but is based on teachers' assessments only.

3. This reflects a complex set of factors, including the partly proportional system used for National Assembly elections.

4. However, the study also identifies a number of problematic areas, especially with respect to the longer-term viability of some courses (especially in vocational areas) (Estyn, 2010).

5. It is, however, instructive that the transformation policy has stopped short of adopting the approach advocated by the Webb Review, which recommended that commissioning consortia should use the WAG's effective control of funding to ensure that strategic policy objectives are delivered (Webb Review, 2007: Chapter 7).

6. The best-known example here is the University of the Heads of the Valleys Initiative in Blaenau Gwent and Merthyr Tydfil (DCELLS, 2009).

7. There is also, of course, a significant European level, which is especially important to the funding of initiatives in areas of significant economic disadvantage. This level is discussed only in passing here.

8. As noted earlier, there are considerable complexities here. Some commentators have argued that the WAG has been very active in building the capacity of some groups – in particular, 'descriptive minorities' such as gay, lesbian and bisexual and black minority ethnic groups – to participate in policy-making processes (for example, Royles, 2007). Accordingly, it is important to emphasize that the arguments here relate specifically to the policy network relating to education and training.

9. For example, even in the consultation on the *Skills That Work for Wales* strategy, where workplace skills play a very significant role, almost 50 per cent of those participating represented these sorts of 'skills producer' interests.

10. It may well be that the extensive experience in Wales of European funding programmes, which generally require a 'social partnership' model, has been influential here.

11. Unless indicated otherwise, all the statistical data in the following are derived from the Statistics Wales website at <http://wales.gov.uk/topics/statistics/?lang=en> (accessed 15 October 2010). The most recent available data are used.

12. Unlike in the regions of England, the funding of public policy in Wales (as in Scotland and Northern Ireland) is not based primarily on measures of current 'social need'. Rather, an annual block grant is allocated to the WAG on the basis of the Barnett Formula. This sets the size of the grants to the devolved administrations in relation to historical levels of public expenditure outside of England, adjusted according to changes in elements of public spending in England and relative population size. There are relatively few restrictions on how the devolved administrations distribute the block grant between the policy areas within their jurisdictions.

References

Adams, J. and Robinson, P. (eds) (2002) *Devolution in Practice: Public policy differences within the UK*. London: Institute for Public Policy Research.

Day, G., Dunkerley, D. and Thompson, A. (eds) (2006) *Civil Society in Wales: Policy, politics and people*. Cardiff: University of Wales Press.

Department for Children, Education, Lifelong Learning and Skills (DCELLS) (2008a) *Skills that Work for Wales: A skills and employment strategy and action plan*. Cardiff: Welsh Assembly Government (WAG).

-- (2008b) *Transforming Education and Training Provision in Wales: Delivering skills that work for Wales*. Cardiff: WAG.

-- (2009) *Transformation: Y Siwrnai: Transforming education and training provision in Wales*. Cardiff: WAG.

Drakeford, M. (2005) 'Wales and a third term of New Labour: Devolution and the development of difference'. *Critical Social Policy*, 25(4), 497–506.

Education and Training Action Group (1999) *An Education and Training Action Plan for Wales*. Cardiff: Welsh Office.

Estyn (2010) *Wider Choice and the Learning Core: Progress in implementing a wider option choice and the learning core for 14–19 learners*. Cardiff: Estyn.

Independent Commission on Funding and Finance for Wales (ICFFW) (Holtham Commission) (2009) *First Report. Funding Devolved Government in Wales: Barnett and beyond*. Cardiff: ICFFW.

Jones, B. and Osmond, J. (2001) *Inclusive Government and Party Management: The National Assembly for Wales and the work of its committees*. Cardiff: Institute for Welsh Affairs and Welsh Governance Centre.

Keep, E. (2008) 'A comparison of the Welsh Workforce Development Programme and England's Train to Gain'. *SKOPE Research Paper 79*, Oxford and Cardiff Universities: SKOPE.

Keep, E., Payne, J. and Rees, G. (2010) 'Devolution and strategies for learning and skills: The Leitch Report and its alternatives'. In G. Lodge and K. Schmuecker (eds), *Devolution in Practice 2010*. London: IPPR.

Leitch, S. (2006) *Prosperity for All in the Global Economy: World class skills*. London: HM Treasury.

Morgan, K. and Mungham, G. (2000) *Redesigning Democracy: The making of the Welsh Assembly*. Bridgend: Seren.

Morgan, K. and Rees, G. (2001) 'Learning by doing: Devolution and the governance of economic development in Wales'. In P. Chaney, T. Hall and

A. Pithouse (eds), *New Governance: New democracy?*. Cardiff: University of Wales Press.

Morgan, K., Rees, G. and Garmise, S. (1999) 'Networking for local economic development'. In G. Stoker (ed.), *Local Governance in Britain*. Basingstoke: Macmillan, in association with the ESRC Local Governance Programme.

Morgan, R. (2002) 'Making social policy in Wales'. Speech to the National Centre for Public Policy. University of Wales, Swansea, 11 December.

National Assembly for Wales (2001) *The Learning Country: A comprehensive education and lifelong learning programme to 2010 in Wales*. Cardiff: National Assembly for Wales.

Paterson, L. (2003) 'The three educational ideologies of the British Labour Party, 1997–2001'. *Oxford Review of Education*, 29(2), 165–86.

PricewaterhouseCoopers (PWC) (2010) *Review of the Cost of Administering the Education System in Wales: Phase 1*. London: PWC.

Rees, G. (2002) 'Devolution and the restructuring of post-16 education and training in the UK'. In J. Adams and P. Robinson (eds), *Devolution in Practice: Public policy differences within the UK*. London: IPPR.

-- (2004) 'Democratic devolution and education policy in Wales: The emergence of a national system?'. *Contemporary Wales*, 17, 28–43.

-- (2007) 'The impacts of parliamentary devolution on education policy in Wales'. *Welsh Journal of Education*, 14(1), 8–20.

Rees, G. and Stroud, D. (2004) 'Regenerating the coalfields: The South Wales experience'. Bevan Foundation Policy Report No. 5. Tredegar: The Bevan Foundation.

Rees, G. and Taylor, C. (2006) 'Devolution and the restructuring of participation in higher education in Wales'. *Higher Education Quarterly*, 60(4), 370–91.

Reynolds, D. (2008) 'New Labour, education and Wales: The devolution decade'. *Oxford Review of Education*, 34(6), 753–65.

Royles, E. (2007) *Revitalizing Democracy? Devolution and civil society in Wales*. Cardiff: University of Wales Press.

Statistics for Wales (2009) 'Employment in the public sector in Wales'. Statistical Bulletin SB 27/2009. Cardiff: Welsh Assembly Government.

UK Commission for Employment and Skills (UKCES) (2009) *Ambition 2020: World class skills and jobs for the UK*. Wath-upon-Dearne: UKCES.

Wales Employment and Skills Board (WESB) (2010) *Moving Forward: Foundations for growth. Volume 1: Economic Renewal and the Skills Agenda.* Cardiff: WESB.

Webb Review (2007) *Promise and Performance: The report of the independent review of the mission and purpose of further education in Wales.* Cardiff: WAG.

Welsh Assembly Government (WAG) (2007) *One Wales: A progressive agenda for the government of Wales.* Cardiff: WAG.

-- (2009) *Update Paper for the Ninth Economic Summit.* Cardiff: WAG.

PART 2

ORGANISATION, GOVERNANCE AND PRACTICE

Chapter 5

Organisational arrangements in England, Scotland and Wales: How the systems work

Ann Hodgson, Ken Spours and Martyn Waring
with Stuart Gardner, Jim Gallacher and Dennis Gunning

A framework of analysis: Political eras and the education state

A description of organisational arrangements for education and training in any particular country provides an important but partial picture. What it cannot show is how policy is formulated and enacted. This chapter attempts to illustrate the dynamics of governance arrangements in the different countries of the UK. We suggest that the relationships between various actors and agencies and the interplay between different levels of the system can be analysed through the concept of the 'education state'. This allows us to explore how organisational and policy relationships are configured, who exercises power and the scope for action by education professionals. We also argue that different national 'versions' of the education state can best be understood as part of a wider historical framework.

According to Hodgson and Spours (2006), the education state can be seen to comprise a range of national, regional and local structures, institutions and key groups or individuals. These include centres of political power (e.g. the Number 10 Policy Unit in England), Parliaments or Assemblies, government departments, regulatory and quality assurance agencies, quasi-autonomous non-governmental organisations (quangos), including funding bodies, regional and local government and public and private education providers. The concept of the education state goes beyond purely governmental institutions to capture the significant role of a set of major players within the contested landscape of education policy (Ball, 1990; Ozga, 2000). Key social partners and education pressure groups, such as professional associations, teacher unions and think tanks, as well as the education media and influential individuals, all of whom exercise different degrees of political power and influence at different points in the policy process, can play a major role within this expanded concept of the education state.

The balance and relationship between all of these components differ in the four countries of the UK. In England and Northern Ireland, for example, there is a greater role for quangos, whereas in Wales local government has retained greater influence and in Scotland the college sector continues to enjoy a prominent position. Each of the three country accounts below will provide examples of different approaches to the organisation of the education state and in the final part of the chapter we will draw out the implications for the way in which education and training policy-making is conducted and shapes the respective systems. While Northern Ireland did not feature as a specific national case in the research seminars, its current approach to policy-making is noted in the final section of this chapter.

It is important to set current models of the education state in each of the countries of the UK within an historical perspective. This allows us to see what was already happening prior to parliamentary devolution, what has taken place since and how these affect the dynamics of education and training policy in the UK. We use the concept of 'political eras' (Hodgson and Spours, 2006), because this locates education policy and structures within a wider historical, socio-economic and political analysis. The term 'political eras' describes a period of politics and policy-making framed by three major factors – underlying societal shifts and historical trends which influence the 'shape' of the education and training system; the dominant political ideology of the time, which affects the parameters for reform; and national and international education debates, which either support or contest the dominant ideology.

Throughout the seminar series that gave rise to this book, policy-makers, researchers and practitioners repeatedly asserted that governance arrangements in England had changed significantly over the past three decades, while in Scotland and Wales they had not. This assertion rests on an analysis that suggests that England has experienced a long political era of neo-liberal reform, beginning in the early 1980s under the Conservatives and arguably continuing in an adapted form under New Labour. Neo-liberalism and its associated reforms, it was claimed, did not take root in the other two countries to the same extent. As a result, the shape and dynamics of the education state changed more dramatically in England than in Wales or Scotland. The three case studies outlined below provide accounts to illustrate the degree to which this assertion holds true.

As we saw in Chapter 1, education policy in England was increasingly centralised and politicised from the early 1980s (Raffe and Spours, 2007). Powers were remorselessly concentrated in the hands of ministers and the Prime Minister, who used arm's-length agencies (e.g. the Learning and Skills Council) and a variety of powerful policy levers (e.g. funding, inspection, targets and performance tables) to influence the behaviour of education institutions. At the same time, individual education providers were given greater autonomy from local government via college incorporation (UK Parliament, 1992) and local management of schools (UK Parliament, 1988). Policy centralisation was accompanied by privatisation and marketisation (Ball, 2007) as private providers (e.g. Tribal) took on roles that would previously have been undertaken by higher education institutions, Her Majesty's Inspectorate and local authority advisory services. At the same time, schools, colleges and independent learning providers were encouraged to compete for learners. Local authorities, education professionals and teacher unions were marginalised in the policy process, particularly at the point of policy formulation (Coffield *et al.*, 2008). Scotland and Wales, on the other hand, while affected by this political era of neo-liberalism prior to devolution, were able to retain a more traditional social democratic approach to policy-making with a greater role for local partners and education professionals (Raffe, 2007). It could be argued that this position has remained or even increased over the last ten years, going some way to explaining key differences between the 'education state' and how it operates in each of the three countries.

The remainder of this chapter contains four sections. The first three describe the organisational arrangements in England, Scotland and Wales respectively, raising issues about the nature and role of the state, the main policy players, the impact of patterns of participation in education and training and the relationship between national, regional and local governance and institutional configurations. Each account highlights implications for the conduct of policy and its effects on learners, educational professionals and wider stakeholders, such as employers. Reflections on these three accounts (also making brief reference to Northern Ireland) form the basis of the final section. Here we reflect on the differing approaches to the education state, the extent to which these have led to greater divergence between the constituent parts of the UK in the provision of post-compulsory education and lifelong learning, and the competing pressures for convergence or divergence in the current political and economic climate.

Organisational arrangements in England
Stuart Gardner

Introduction

This account describes the organisation of post-compulsory education and training in England at government level and the intermediaries between government and local authorities or learning providers. It covers a period of significant investment in education and training, both for young people (aged 16–19) and adults (aged 19+), during which participation in learning by young people reached the highest levels ever and there was a major shift in the focus of state support for adult learning.

Current structural and organisational arrangements

The organisation of the post-compulsory education and training system in England in the period 1997 to 2010 saw numerous changes at government level. The Labour Party was in government throughout that period, until the general election of May 2010, which resulted in a Conservative–Liberal Democrat Coalition Government. In 1997, all post-16 education and training policy fell under the Department for Education and Employment (DfEE); this covered all learning in schools, further education and sixth form colleges, higher education institutions, local authority adult education and private training providers.

In 2001, the employment functions were transferred to a newly created Department for Work and Pensions (DWP), with the DfEE becoming the Department for Education and Skills (DfES). In 2007, the DfES was split into two new departments; the Department for Children, Schools and Families (DCSF), which was responsible for education and training up to the age of 19, and the Department for Innovation, Universities and Skills (DIUS), with responsibility for education and training post-19.

In 2009, DIUS was renamed the Department for Business, Innovation and Skills (BIS), taking on additional responsibilities, and in 2010, following the change in government, DCSF was renamed the Department for Education (DfE).

Whilst the responsibility for policy was at departmental level, the planning and funding of education was delivered through intermediaries. In 1997, the planning and funding of post-16 education (other than higher education) was the responsibility of the Further Education Funding Council (FEFC), a non-departmental public body; at the same time, training came under the aegis of some 72 Training and Enterprise Councils (TECs) across England, all of which were established as private companies, usually limited by guarantee.

In 2001, the functions of the FEFC and the TECs were merged into a new non-departmental public body, the Learning and Skills Council (LSC), and in 2010, the LSC was abolished and three new bodies were established: the Young People's Learning Agency (YPLA), a non-departmental public body; the Skills Funding Agency (SFA), an executive agency within BIS; and the National Apprenticeship Service (NAS), a service within the SFA.

The inspection regime has been subject to less change over the period from 1997, but has not been entirely immune. Throughout that period, school sixth forms have been inspected by Ofsted, a non-ministerial government department. Private training providers were inspected by the Training Standards Council (TSC) and colleges, including sixth form colleges and local authority adult education services, were inspected by the FEFC. In 2001, the FEFC's responsibilities for the inspection of education up to the age of 19 transferred to Ofsted, and its responsibilities for the inspection of training for those over the age of 16 and for adult education moved to the newly formed Adult Learning Inspectorate (ALI), which also took over the TSC's responsibilities. For most further education colleges, this meant that inspections were undertaken jointly by Ofsted and ALI, until 2007, when the latter was abolished and its responsibilities transferred to Ofsted, which thus became responsible for the inspection of all education and training in England.

For 16–18 year olds, the DfE Secretary of State publishes an annual grant letter setting out the funding available and key priorities for that funding. The YPLA allocates funding on behalf of the Secretary of State for young people in school sixth forms and academies, sixth form colleges, general further education colleges, independent training providers and for young offender institutions. For adult provision, the BIS Secretary of State publishes annually a skills investment strategy, setting out the funding available and the planned numbers of learners across a range of programmes. The SFA works with colleges, training providers and employers to agree allocations to each of those providers and, on behalf of the DfE, works with local authorities on 16–19 Apprenticeships. The SFA also has responsibilities for performance management of the providers it funds. The NAS works directly with employers to ensure that sufficient Apprenticeship places are available (see Figure 5.1).

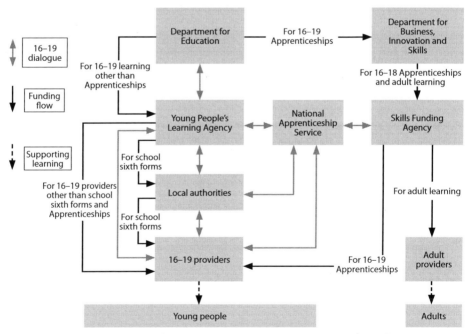

Figure 5.1: Governance of post-compulsory education and training and lifelong learning

The providers

State-funded post-compulsory education and training is delivered by a wide variety of providers, but primarily by further education colleges (including sixth form colleges and a range of specialist colleges such as land-based), schools, private training organisations (including charitable organisations and for-profit businesses), employers and local authorities (for adult education). The pattern of provision varies widely across the country, with some areas having sixth forms in all their schools, others having sixth form colleges and general further education colleges, and others having tertiary colleges, which provide all learning post-16 for the area. In most areas, however, the picture is more mixed, with some schools having sixth forms in areas with sixth form colleges. Between them, in 2008–09, these providers delivered education and training to over 4.8 million learners, of whom just under 1.5 million were aged 16–19.

The learners were spread between those different providers broadly as indicated in Table 5.1.

Table 5.1: Distribution of learners between providers (2008–09)

Type of provider	Number of learners
Further education colleges	2,700,000
Schools	400,000
Private training providers and employers (work-based learning)	1,150,000
Local authority adult education	630,000

In addition, some 120,000 learners, distributed throughout the system, were on provision supported by the European Social Fund (LSC, 2008).

The figures above relate only to those young people and adults whose learning was supported by state funding. Whilst detailed numbers are not known, a significant number of adult learners fund their own learning on provision which either does not lead to a qualification or where the qualification is not eligible for funding. Finally, around 200,000 overseas students (i.e. from outside the European Economic Area) enter the UK annually for study purposes, studying higher education, further education and at language schools (Hansard, 2009).

Participation rates in education and training by young people aged 16 and 17 showed little change in the period 1997 to 2005, at around 84 per cent of the cohort: by 2009 the rate had risen to 92 per cent (DCSF, 2008). Other than around 6 per cent of the cohort who were in independent schools, those learners were fully funded by the state. Underneath the headline figures, the proportion of those in part-time learning fell from 8.3 per cent in 1997 to 4.5 per cent in 2008, although that figure is expected to rise as more young people in employment undertake part-time learning as the age of compulsory participation is raised.

Key debates

The organisation of learning providers

The wide variety of ways in which post-16 learning providers are organised in different local authorities in England reflects an apparent reluctance on the part of the national government to become involved in planning at local level.

The FEFC was, as its name implies, a funding council, whose primary function was to fund the strategic plans of further education colleges. The remit letter to the LSC from the Secretary of State, stated that, 'For the first time, the planning and funding of all post-compulsory learning below higher education will be integrated' (DfEE, 2000), and one of its first actions was to begin strategic area reviews of provision, to identify gaps and overlaps and, by implication, to take action to fill the gaps and remove duplication of provision. One of the early outcomes of those reviews was a proposal in late 2003 by the LSC to close school sixth forms in Carlisle and to replace them with a sixth form college. That proposal led to a storm of protest and an adjournment debate in the House of Commons, and was subsequently withdrawn. Shortly afterwards, the DfES announced that there should be a 'strong presumption' that successful and popular specialist schools should be allowed to develop new sixth forms. The LSC's planning role seemed to be over as far as schools were concerned. Strategic area reviews also covered provision for young people in further education colleges and with training providers. Structural changes to those providers are always less contentious than for schools, but even so any changes were relatively minor and responded to demand from the providers, with no strong national steer from ministers.

One major change has been the introduction from 2002 of academies, state-funded but independent schools, with the programme introduced primarily to replace underperforming secondary schools, mainly in deprived areas. By 2010, there were over 200 academies, with ministers at the time expressing an aspiration for that number to rise to 400, which would be over 10 per cent of all secondary schools in England. The first Act introduced by the Coalition Government in May 2010 sought to expand the programme greatly, to include high-performing secondary schools, as well as primary and special schools, with the Secretary of State, Michael Gove, stating that he expected most schools to become academies.

The curriculum for young people

In terms of the curriculum for young people, recent years have seen a continuation of a debate that has been going on for over a century – the place of vocational education and training in the curriculum. A major review of the curriculum for 14–19 year olds, chaired by Mike (now Sir Mike) Tomlinson, recommended that the existing framework of qualifications for young people should be replaced by a single framework of Diplomas, with qualifications such as the General Certificate of Secondary Education (GCSE) and the General Certificate of Education Advanced

Level (GCE A Level) examinations being withdrawn. These Diplomas would all involve a significant element of applied learning, and the recommendations envisaged that they should, ultimately, incorporate Apprenticeships (Working Group on 14–19 Reform, 2004). The Government did not accept the Tomlinson recommendations in full, but instead introduced a set of Diplomas alongside GCSEs and GCE A Levels and other existing qualifications for 14–19 year olds.

In December 2008, the Secretary of State for Children, Schools and Families established the Joint Advisory Committee for Qualifications Approval (JACQA), to be jointly chaired by the LSC and the Qualifications and Curriculum Development Agency, with a remit to keep under review the funding eligibility of qualifications. The aim was that, by 2013, the qualifications offer for 14–19 year olds should be based on four learning routes of Apprenticeships, Diplomas, Foundation Learning and general qualifications (GCSEs and GCE A Levels). For a qualification to be eligible for public funding, all that was required was that the awarding organisation should meet certain criteria, and so should the qualification itself. In its first report, setting the baseline, JACQA found that over 300 awarding organisations offered between them over 18,000 qualifications that were eligible for funding for 14–19 year olds, of which some 12,500 qualifications had no 14–19 year old enrolments and a further 3,500 had less than 100 (LSC, 2010). JACQA recommended that by August 2012 public funding should be withdrawn from such qualifications. In November 2010, the Government announced that JACQA would be dissolved and that there would be a review of the need for any replacement committee (see <www.education.gov.uk/section96/>).

Funding provision for adults

Before 2001, funding for adult education and training was split between local authorities (for adult and community learning), TECs (for work-based learning) and the FEFC (for provision in colleges). Data on student numbers, even where they were collected, were not collated centrally.

These three strands were brought together in 2001 with the creation of the LSC. At that time there was an expectation that, for adult learners, either they or their employer would contribute 25 per cent of the cost of their learning, except for those on a range of benefits and for basic skills learners. From 2003, and in particular with the publication of the Leitch Report on Skills (Leitch, 2006), government policy on adult education came to focus on improving the skills of the adult workforce. Fee remission was extended to cover adults studying for their first full Level 2 qualification (at the equivalent of five GCSE grades A*–C) and those aged 19–25 studying for their first full Level 3 qualification (at the equivalent of two GCE A Levels), and at the same time the assumed fee level was increased incrementally towards a figure of 50 per cent from 2010–11. The combined effect of those changes saw an estimated fall in the numbers of adults on programmes for personal and community development learning, which was often not qualification-based, from 840,000 in 2003–04 to 585,000 in 2010–11 (House of Commons, 2009).

In 2007, the LSC introduced new funding models which split the funding for adult learning into three distinct elements (LSC, 2007). Personal and community development learning was renamed 'adult safeguarded learning', which reflected a commitment to maintain the funding level, although without any increase to reflect inflation this meant that learner numbers would continue to fall. The remaining budget was split between 'adult responsive' (responding to demand from adults for personal development programmes) and 'employer responsive' (responding to demand from employers), with an investment strategy for the period 2008–09 to 2010–11 which would see the numbers of learners on 'adult responsive' learning fall from 1.45 million to 1.12 million while those on 'employer responsive' learning would rise from 1.43 million to 1.72 million (BIS, 2009).

Future direction of policy

History suggests that there will be further significant changes in organisational structures at government and intermediary level, but little at local authority or institutional level. The new departmental arrangements have not had time to demonstrate whether they are working effectively, but there are tensions in a system in which many further education colleges receive the majority of their funding from the YPLA, while the performance management of those colleges is the responsibility of the SFA.

The JACQA work on reviewing existing qualifications for young people and the national rollout of Diplomas are both taking place in the context of ensuring that suitable qualifications are available to enable all young people to remain in learning until at least age 18. The main uncertainties in this area are around the level of take-up of Diplomas (and of their acceptance by employers and higher education) and how young people in employment will undertake the required part-time learning.

For adults the general direction of policy seems set to continue, with increasing government emphasis on skills for the workforce. It is likely that this will be accompanied by a growing expectation of a greater contribution from employers to the learning of their workforce.

Organisational arrangements in Scotland
Jim Gallacher

The policy context

It has been noted in Chapter 3 that there have been two significant phases of policy development in lifelong learning in Scotland in recent years.

The first phase occurred after the UK election of a New Labour Government in 1997, and the establishment of the Scottish Parliament in 1999. Under these devolutionary arrangements the funding and national governance structures increasingly began to diverge from those found in England. An important characteristic of the policy framework in Scotland has been the extent to which lifelong learning continued to be a key aspect of the policy agenda, while in England it was increasingly being replaced by a growing emphasis on skills. Associated with this emphasis on lifelong learning, there has been a strong stress on collaboration. These approaches are designed to facilitate the development of a more seamless tertiary education system, in which there will be more opportunities for learners to move between different parts, thus widening the range of learning opportunities available.

A second policy phase can be recognised as having been introduced when a minority Scottish National Party (SNP) Government was elected in 2007. This government has placed greater emphasis on skills, associated with its political agenda of establishing sustainable economic growth, which would underpin an independent Scotland. There has also been a continued recognition of the importance of the wider aspects of lifelong learning, which is now seen as something stretching from 'cradle to grave'. The focus is no longer just on post-compulsory education.

The organisational context

The policy context outlined above, with its emphasis on lifelong learning and collaboration as central pillars, has supported the emergence of a number of organisations and initiatives, which have helped shape the landscape.

First, the establishment of a joint funding council for further and higher education can be noted as a development of considerable significance. The Scottish Further Education Funding Council (SFEFC) had been established in 1999, to sit alongside the Scottish Higher Education Funding Council (SHEFC), with the responsibility for funding and supporting the work of the Scottish colleges. However in 2005, following a recommendation from the Scottish Parliament's Inquiry into Lifelong Learning (Scottish Parliament, 2002), the Scottish Funding Council for Further and Higher Education (SFC) was established. The legislation to create the new council made clear that an important objective was to develop a more cohesive and effective system of tertiary education in Scotland. It has put in place a national framework for the governance of the college sector in Scotland, which is now quite different from that which exists in England and in many other parts of the world.

Different funding methodologies operate for the colleges and the higher education institutions (HEIs), but an important feature of the Scottish system is that all funding for both further and higher education courses goes directly to the colleges. This differs from the more complex system in England, which often involves indirect funding. Associated with this, English colleges have been subject to greater fluctuation and insecurity in their funding (Parry, 2009). These arrangements have enabled Scottish colleges to develop as a robust and confident sector, which provides a wide range of lifelong learning opportunities from adult basic education to degree level.

A second and more recent collaborative development has been the establishment of Skills Development Scotland (SDS) in 2008. This can be seen as an expression of the interest of the SNP Government in pursuing its agenda for the establishment of a sustainable economic base for Scotland. This body was created by bringing together the national training programmes funded by Scottish Enterprise and Highlands and Islands Enterprise, Careers Scotland and the Scottish University for Industry. It now has responsibility for a wide range of skills development related activities. These include Modern Apprenticeships, information advice and guidance, literacy and numeracy campaigns, and financial support for part-time learners through Individual Learning Accounts (ILAs). Its budget for 2010–11 is £198.2 million. The provision of an all-age information, advice and guidance service, and of financial support through ILAs, is an important feature of the Scottish system, although these initiatives predated the establishment of SDS.

A third organisation, which has been of major significance in shaping the provision of post-compulsory education and lifelong learning, is the Scottish Qualifications Authority (SQA). This was established in 1998 through the merger of the Scottish Examinations Board, which was responsible for the school-based qualifications (Highers and Standard Grades), and the Scottish Vocational Education Council, which had responsibility for college-based and work-based qualifications (National Certificates, Higher National Certificates and Diplomas (HNC/Ds), and Scottish Vocational Qualifications (SVQs)). A further distinctive aspect of the Scottish system of post-compulsory education and lifelong learning is, therefore, that it now has one body which is responsible for developing, validating and awarding all qualifications, both 'vocational' and 'academic', other than those conferred by the universities.

The fourth organisation that has been important in attempting to create a more coordinated system of education and training is the Scottish Credit and Qualifications Framework (SCQF), established in 2001 with cooperation from stakeholder bodies. As a result of their involvement, all the main qualifications in Scotland have now been credit rated and included in the SCQF. A considerable volume of work has also been undertaken to include systems for the recognition of prior learning within the framework. The aim has been to create a more flexible lifelong learning system and to ensure that people find it easier to gain credit for any learning they have undertaken and to move from one part of the education and lifelong learning system to another.

A fifth organisation influencing developments in both the school and college sectors is Her Majesty's Inspectorate of Education (HMIE). The role of HMIE as the main agency for quality assurance in both the school and college sectors has been maintained in Scotland, although it became an independent executive agency in 2001. This can be seen as another example of the more evolutionary change in Scotland when compared with other parts of the UK. The Inspectorate is not only responsible for quality assurance in schools and colleges, but also has an important role in the development of educational policy and practice in both sectors.

These five organisations can, therefore, be seen as creating the national framework within which post-compulsory education and lifelong learning is being provided within Scotland. All these organisations are in some sense new, in that they have been created since 1997 and, with the exception of SQA, have been established post-devolution. However, they can also be seen to represent an evolutionary process of change, which builds on earlier developments and organisations, and in which the encouragement of collaboration to create a more integrated system has been an important element.

The providers

The main providers of post-compulsory education and lifelong learning, apart from the HEIs, are Scotland's Colleges. These are now known by this name rather than as 'further education (FE) colleges', reflecting the fact that they all provide a significant amount of higher education (HE) level work, which averages around 10 per cent. They presently number 43 and will receive £690 million in funding from the SFC in 2010–11. Many of these colleges can be seen as 'community colleges' in that they provide a wide range of courses for the communities they serve. One indication of this role is the age range covered; just under half of all students (49 per cent) are aged 25 or over, while a third are in the 16–24 age group (SFC, 2010a).

There are also a number of more specialist colleges, including land-based and city-centre colleges, such as the Glasgow College of Nautical Studies, although these specialist focuses will also be combined with more general provision. Unlike in England, there are no sixth form colleges and while many institutions will provide opportunities for students to study for SQA Highers (the main school-leaving qualification), the extent of this provision is limited (to around 2 per cent of all students). However, a schools/college initiative was established by the Scottish Executive in 2005 to encourage cooperation between schools and colleges, and provide additional learning opportunities for school-aged pupils (Scottish Executive, 2005). Associated with this, 19 per cent of college students are under the age of 16. Table 5.2 provides an overview of participation in Scotland's Colleges over the past ten years.

Table 5.2 Qualification aim of study in Scotland's Colleges 1998–99 and 2008–09

	1998–99		2008–09	
FE	350,446	(83%)	435,117	(90%)
HE	71,110	(17%)	48,355	(10%)
Total	421,556	(100%)	483,472	(100%)

Source: SFC, 2010b

It can be noted that the overwhelming majority of students (around 90 per cent) are on FE level courses and these numbers have continued to increase over the past ten years. However, only 10 per cent of these students are full-time, compared with the 54 per cent of HE level students, so the contribution of FE level students to full-time equivalent student numbers in colleges is much lower. Given that we have suggested that many of these colleges can be seen as 'community colleges', it is not surprising that the FE level courses cover a very wide range of provision. This includes courses offering the first steps towards returning to education and ones which provide opportunities to progress to higher level study. Colleges also have a significant role in the provision of S/NVQs, which are work-based qualifications. A growth of SVQs at Level 3 has been associated with the increase in Modern Apprenticeships over this period. Apprentices registered on these programmes rose from around 10,000 in 2000–01 to over 26,000 in 2008–09 (SDS, 2010). However, while S/NVQs are an important part of the vocational provision at FE level in the colleges, they accounted for just 6.4 per cent of all students in 2008–09. It can also be noted that a fairly large proportion of students (41 per cent) are on courses which do not lead to any recognised qualification, although almost all of these students are part-time. In a number of cases these courses will be developed in cooperation with local authority community learning and development staff and will be provided in community settings.

Table 5.2 also shows that in 2008–09, 10 per cent of students were on HE level courses. However, as a result of the relatively high numbers of full-time students in this group, HE level courses are a much more significant aspect of college provision than these headline figures might suggest. HE provision in the Scottish colleges differs from England and other parts of the UK in significant ways. In the first place, with 21 per cent of all undergraduate level students in Scotland studying in the colleges, they account for a relatively high proportion of HE level students overall (Scottish Government, 2010). Second, almost all of this provision has been for qualifications developed and validated under the auspices of SQA. In 2008–09, students on SQA HNC/Ds accounted for 82 per cent of those on HE courses, while those on degrees accounted for only about 1 per cent (SFC, 2010b). Franchising or other forms of partnerships with the universities have not been a feature of this growth of HE in the college sector, and Foundation Degrees have not been developed as a policy initiative in Scotland. However, the figures also show that there has been a significant decline in the numbers of HE level students in the colleges over the past ten years.

While the colleges are the main providers of post-compulsory education and lifelong learning, there is another significant group of training providers, which operate mainly in the private sector, although they also include employers in both the public and private sectors. It is difficult to obtain accurate, systematic and up-to-date data about these providers. Osborne and Turner (2002) have offered an analysis of the role of private training providers (PTPs) in Scotland based on data provided by SQA and City and Guilds for the period 1996–97 to 1998–99. From this they identified around 300 PTPs and around 19,000 students who were registered with them. By 2008–09 there were over 25,000 students registered for SVQs awarded by SQA with a range of training providers, employers and others, and a further 12,000 registered for VQs awarded by other agencies. This gave a total of just over 37,000 candidates for VQs registered with organisations other than colleges, a figure considerably in excess of the 32,500 registered in the colleges. The role of these training providers within the vocational education and training sector in Scotland is therefore of considerable importance.

Key issues and challenges

As has been indicated above, Scotland has seen a process of evolutionary change in which successive political administrations have encouraged greater collaboration between agencies to create a more coherent system of lifelong learning, with an increasing emphasis on skills utilisation in the period since 2007. However, questions remain regarding the impact of these policies and these help to define some of the issues and challenges for the future.

The first set of questions relates to the arrangements for the funding, governance and planning of post-compulsory education and lifelong learning in Scotland. We have noted above that the SFC was established in 2005 with a responsibility for the funding of all further and higher education in Scotland, and a remit to ensure that a more coherent system of tertiary education is developed. We have also noted that SDS has been established more recently with a remit to develop the skills agenda in a more effective way. Part of this remit is to fund the Modern Apprenticeship programme in Scotland, and many of these apprentices attend college as part of their training. At present there is a joint skills committee for SFC and SDS, but an important question for the future will be how these two national organisations can work together to ensure that post-compulsory education and lifelong learning is provided most effectively and an appropriate skills strategy is implemented. This will have implications for identifying the skills needed in a changing economic context and the training needed to provide these skills, requiring all organisations to work even more collaboratively.

The contribution of the SCQF to the facilitation of change and collaboration that can open up new opportunities for learners will also remain a challenging issue. While Scotland is now recognised as an international leader in having established such a comprehensive national credit and qualifications framework, it is not yet clear whether it is having the desired impact in creating more flexibility in the system. It has been suggested that it must be complemented by other policies, which motivate people to use the potential that the framework provides (Raffe *et al.*, 2008).

The third set of issues relates to curriculum, programmes and qualifications. The Curriculum for Excellence (CfE) is a major review of the curriculum for young people aged 3–18. This is designed to develop skills for learning, life and work. While this has its origins in school-based education, it is recognised that the senior phase of the CfE will have a significant impact on colleges as well as on schools, and the national qualifications framework which provides most of the FE level qualifications in the colleges is being reviewed as part of this process.

With respect to HE level qualifications, we have noted above the continuing importance of HNC/Ds. However, issues also exist here regarding the current role of these qualifications and the possible need for change. While some continue to be used primarily as vocational qualifications, a number are now used as transitional qualifications to enable progression to bachelors degrees (Ingram *et al.*, 2009). This has been associated with a change in the balance of HNC/Ds away from HNCs, which were predominantly part-time and aimed at people who were often in employment and wished to improve their qualifications, to HNDs which are mainly full-time and attract higher numbers of younger students who often use these qualifications as routes into further study (Gallacher, 2009). Comparative research has also shown that, as a result of national policy initiatives, work-based learning has a more significant role in Foundation Degrees in England than in many HNC/Ds in Scotland (Gallacher *et al.*, 2009). There is also evidence of the growth in corporate qualifications, such as those provided by Cisco and Microsoft. While a major review and modernisation programme for HNC/Ds has been undertaken in recent years, it would appear that further work is required to ensure that these qualifications are well suited to meet that range of roles which they now have. This may involve enhancing the vocational aspects of some, and in particular considering how they can better meet the needs of part-time, work-based students. In other cases it may be to recognise that they are essentially transitional qualifications and to consider how the linkages between these programmes, and the bachelors degrees to which they give access, can be enhanced.

The fourth set of issues relates to the provision of financial support for people enrolled on these programmes and particularly for part-time students. There is a complex system of bursaries, loans and fee-waivers for full-time students, but most of these do not apply to part-time students. As we have indicated above, some progress has been made in this area with the reintroduction of ILAs. However, questions regarding the ways and extent to which support should be provided for part-time learners, and whether the idea of an entitlement could be introduced, still exist. In particular, issues regarding the role of employers in supporting the training of their employees, and the dangers of deadweight if additional public funding is provided, are important. These will need to be addressed if equitable opportunities for access to education and training are to be available to part-time learners.

While the questions identified above are ones which create important challenges for the development of post-compulsory education and lifelong learning in Scotland, they will now have to be addressed in the context of the severe spending cuts which will be imposed following the Spending Review in the autumn of 2010. It is clear that the Scottish Government and the SFC will be seeking new and innovative ways of providing education and training to ensure that more can be done with less. This imperative is likely to encourage the search for more radical solutions to some of these challenges.

Organisational arrangements in Wales
Dennis Gunning

Structural and organisational arrangements

Devolution to Wales is ten years young. Since the devolved government was set up, a range of national strategic documents such as *Wales: A Vibrant Economy* (National Assembly for Wales, 2005) and *The Learning Country* (National Assembly for Wales, 2001) were produced by the Welsh Assembly Government (WAG) to set the future direction in the economy and in education and training. More recently, from 2007 a coalition government involving the Welsh Labour Party and Plaid Cymru has been working to a four-year programme, *One Wales* (WAG, 2007), which drew on previous strategic directions and signalled a focus on high employment, distinctive approaches in education and training, Welsh language development and social justice. These approaches have more recently had to be adapted to the very different economic environment of the global recession.

A single executive department, the Department for Children, Education, Lifelong Learning and Skills (DCELLS), has responsibility for education and training in Wales. Its budget for funding of post-16 courses in school sixth forms, further education, higher education, work-based learning, adult community learning and for bespoke skills development for businesses in Wales was around £1 billion in 2010–11. Although employment policy is not devolved, DCELLS has close and positive relationships with the UK Department for Work and Pensions and its Jobcentre Plus delivery arm in Wales.

Unlike in other parts of the United Kingdom, almost all non-departmental public bodies (quangos) have been absorbed into the DCELLS; the Higher Education Funding Council for Wales (HEFCW) and the inspectorate for all education except higher education, Estyn, currently remain as separate public bodies, although both have close working relationships with DCELLS and work to annual ministerial remit letters. In the absence of quangos, therefore, DCELLS is responsible for both policy and delivery and must maintain a close and direct relationship with stakeholders and deliverers.

Although responsibility for qualifications regulation lies within DCELLS and there is a distinctive Welsh qualifications framework – the Credit and Qualifications Framework for Wales – FE colleges and work-based learning providers in Wales operate within the English awarding body system. For schools there is a choice, with the Welsh Joint Education Committee being a long-standing, Wales-based, school awarding body, which also now has sole responsibility for the Welsh Baccalaureate Qualification (see Chapter 4 for more details of this qualification).

One of the most important features of the education and training system in Wales is its size. With small numbers of local authorities, FE colleges and universities, and an almost complete absence of quangos, there can be easy communication and direct relationships between providers and the WAG. Such direct lines of communication and regular contact have the advantages of ensuring that messages are not mediated through layers of organisation or bureaucracy, reducing the chance of policy being divorced from the real world and ensuring that the mutual accountability and dependency between the WAG, stakeholders and providers are reinforced.

Twenty-two elected local authorities deliver school education, funded by a WAG grant; there are few schools in Wales outside the local authority service, making school sector organisation in Wales much more similar to Scotland than to England. FE institutions (which statutorily include the Workers' Educational Association and the YMCA) are not run by the local authorities. Instead, they are corporations with boards of governors, with over 70 per cent of their funding being provided by the WAG. Universities in Wales, too, are autonomous institutions governed by university councils set up under Acts of Parliament. They receive around 40 per cent of their funding from the WAG.

The WAG funded 84 providers to deliver work-based learning courses (Apprenticeships and Skillbuild programmes) in 2009–10, of which around three quarters are independent training providers (some run by local authorities and by voluntary bodies, some run as for-profit businesses) and the remainder are FE colleges. A variety of providers also run bespoke post-16 provision, much of which is paid for by learners and/or employers on a fee-for-service basis.

The representative bodies of the sectors, ColegauCymru for FE colleges, the National Training Federation Wales for work-based learning, and Higher Education Wales are among DCELLS's key stakeholder bodies.

The environment for learners: Challenges and policy responses

The learner population in Wales has seen similar demographic trends as the rest of the United Kingdom. Wales has a total population of around three million (5 per cent of the UK); the falling birth rate, which was a pattern of the 1980s and 1990s, is now particularly noticeable in the education system, where the age cohort size has shrunk from over 45,000 in the post-war years and in the late 1960s to a low of 30,000 for those born in 2002. Although the birth rate has been increasing since then, the rate of increase is relatively low. The reduced birth rates of the 1990s will lead to significantly lower numbers of potential 16–18 year old learners for a number of years to come.

At the same time as learner numbers have fallen because of demography, participation and success rates in Wales in the post-compulsory years have been increasing. This has been fuelled partly by new strategies such as the 14–19 Learning Pathways programme and the Welsh Baccalaureate Qualification, and partly by drives to improve the quality of delivery. For example, there have been major improvements in the completion rates of Apprenticeships and in inspection outcomes for Welsh FE colleges and work-based learning providers. More recently, one of the effects of the recession has been to increase the demand for places in post-16 provision. Adult participation in education and training in Wales has also been supported by all-age policy directions adopted in Wales, including Apprenticeships, careers services and basic skills strategies.

There were 251,575 learners at FE institutions, adult community learning and work-based learning providers during 2008–09. In FE, there has been an upward trend in the proportion of full-time learners and a downward trend in the number of those studying part-time. There were more learners aged 16–17 in FE than in secondary schools; the proportion of learners below the age of 25 rose to 38 per cent in FE and 50 per cent in work-based learning (Statistical Directorate, 2009a, 2009b and 2010).

Despite the progress that has been made in Wales since devolution, the challenges to the education and training system remain considerable. Declining employment in the traditional industries such as mining and engineering in South Wales, land-based industry in rural Wales and the tourism industry in rural and coastal Wales has created cycles of inter-generational unemployment and deprivation which are proving hard to break. Although great efforts have been made to attract inward investment, Wales continues to have few corporate headquarters or research and development departments, and although job creation has countered job losses in those traditional industries, growth sectors have often been in areas such as retail, which generate part-time rather than full-time employment opportunities.

Wales has, therefore, remained a relatively low-income part of the UK and has been qualifying for considerable financial support from European Union convergence and competitiveness funding. The long-established link between levels of poverty and educational achievement make it unsurprising, therefore, that Wales has emerged poorly from international benchmarks such as the PISA tests of literacy, numeracy and science and from measures of literacy and numeracy levels in the adult population.

The long-term policy response to these challenges has been to create a major set of reform programmes in the school sector, focusing on the early years, on school effectiveness and on curriculum choice at 14–19, including the further development and expansion of the Welsh Baccalaureate. Taken together, these reforms seek to raise attainment levels of future school-leaving cohorts and, therefore, to minimise the need for remediation in the post-compulsory years through initiatives such as basic skills programmes for adults and Skillbuild for youth and adult unemployed. At the current time, though, such programmes still remain a necessary part of the WAG's investment in education and training.

Policy response for the post-school sectors aimed to take account of the needs of the Welsh labour market, but also to reflect the relatively low levels of educational achievement and high levels of inter-generational poverty that continue to affect parts of Wales. A distinctive skills strategy, *Skills that Work for Wales* (DCELLS, 2008a), was developed which drew on both demand-side and supply-side analyses such as the Leitch (Leitch, 2006) and Webb (Webb Review, 2007) reports and explicitly aimed to cover business development, skills and employment. The connection between skills development and economic development has been reinforced by the 2010 Economic Renewal policy paper (DE&T, 2010), and this is likely to lead to a greater focus within the *Skills that Work for Wales* strategy on skills development that supports economic renewal, the engagement and employment chances of young people and the re-employment of those who have been unemployed.

Key debates

Education and training at the time of devolution had differences from England that reflected the different social values of the Welsh system, such as commitment to comprehensive schooling. These were outweighed by the similarities, given that legislation passed in the UK Parliament prior to devolution in 1999 usually covered both England and Wales. Since devolution,

Wales-specific responses to policy issues have been developed, such as the introduction of the Welsh Baccalaureate Qualification and the abolition of national Key Stage testing. More generally, though, emerging policy differences continue to reflect distinctive Welsh traditions and values, including the importance of the Welsh language, for which a Welsh-medium education strategy has been developed (DCELLS, 2010).

Collaboration and integration

There is a strong political desire in Wales to see education and training based on collaboration rather than competition. This is reflected in the development of collaborative 'effectiveness frameworks' for both school and post-school providers and in the publication of a *Transformation Framework* (DCELLS, 2008b) through which proposals for change to the configuration of post-16 provision were sought. These proposals, which are covered in more detail in Chapter 4, aim to increase learner choice, especially vocational choice, reduce duplication and ensure that the maximum amount of public funding for education is deployed in learning and teaching. The Framework expects regional collaboration in which the interests of learners, not the interests of providers, are paramount.

For the 14–19 age group, the Transformation Framework will support the policy intention of the National Assembly for Wales's Learning and Skills Measure (National Assembly for Wales, 2009), which is designed to attract young people to stay on in education and training by the relevance of the curriculum options available to them, rather than because they are required to do so by legislation to raise the age of statutory participation, as in England. Other potential barriers to collaboration between schools and FE have been removed in support of the 14–19 agenda. For example, Wales has implemented pay parity between FE lecturers and secondary school teachers and has introduced a single, credit-based funding methodology for all non-HE post-16 courses and providers.

A similar direction has been signalled on HE in Wales in the new *For our Future* (DCELLS, 2009) strategy, published in late 2009, where there is political support for much stronger collaboration, at regional and national level, between HE institutions, FE institutions, employers and communities. More recently, reviews of the governance of FE and HE institutions have been set up and these are expected to report in early 2011 (National Assembly for Wales, 2010a and 2010b).

Skills development led by business need

The integration of business development and skills in Wales has been reflected in the close working relationship between the WAG Department for the Economy and Transport and DCELLS, for example in the development of skills interventions that are directed towards specific business needs. Thus, the Workforce Development Programme is an individualised approach to skills development that links the training to the employer's business plan and in which employers applying for funding must commit to match-funding the cost of training. The programme has supported many thousands of businesses and generates very high levels of customer satisfaction.

The tailored approach of the Workforce Development Programme has also been a feature of the skills responses designed to counter the effects of the recent economic downturn in Wales. The existing ReAct (redundancy action plan) programme, which helps a redundant worker to further develop his or her skills base, was scaled up and the innovative ProAct programme, which offers skills development to employees on short-time working, introduced. Both are extensively supported by European funding. ProAct has attracted considerable national and international interest (e.g. New York Times, 2009). In addition, leadership and management training, the Skillbuild employability programme, the Wales TUC redundancy rapid response programme, Careers Wales activity and the basic skills Employer Pledge were all scaled up, and a 'pathways to apprenticeship' programme introduced. When the economic recovery in Wales is secure, support for skills development will be refocused away from counter-recession measures and towards employers with growth potential.

Since 2001, the number of highly skilled jobs in Wales has increased and this trend is expected to continue. The largest expected growth in employment across the UK between now and 2017 will be among the more highly skilled occupational groups, such as management, professionals and associate professional and technical occupations. Nevertheless, the lower end of the labour market will remain a significant source of jobs, especially for people seeking to move out of unemployment or to supplement their income with part-time work. The need to encourage the creation of job opportunities at all skill levels has been emphasised by the Wales Employment and Skills Board (WESB) in its second annual report. WESB sees 'good jobs' as being defined not by whether they are low-skill or high-skill but by whether they are of a kind that will provide progression opportunities, improve economic performance and break the cycle of poverty (WESB, 2010).

Future policy direction

If the direction and momentum of the past few years are maintained, the probability is that the differentiation in policy between Wales and the rest of the UK will increase. There are, however, interesting political times ahead, both at UK and devolved administration level, and it is very difficult to predict how those political events will affect the approach taken by the government in Wales, whatever its political colour, or mix of colours, after the Assembly elections in May 2011.

The current policy directions in Wales will lead to greater integration of both skills, employment and business development services and of governance, planning, funding and delivery between school, FE, HE and work-based learning providers. There will be more priority-driven funding of providers and a greater proportion of the cost of post-19 learning will probably have to be borne by learners and employers.

The long period of relative political stability in Wales has been based on the core values of a left-leaning democracy and has proved resistant to reformist zeal on either side of the political spectrum. There is support for public governance of the education system, for an egalitarian education system, and for collaborative approaches to public services.

The economic downturn showed again how important learning and skills are as investments in the future economic success of Wales and that an education and training system could respond quickly to an emergency. The challenge ahead will be to manage the combination of higher levels of expectation created by that response, greater awareness among employers of the importance of skills development as the basis for growth, and more interest among young people in staying on in education and training – all occurring at a time when the need to reduce the serious UK budget deficit will almost certainly lead to significant and ongoing cuts in public expenditure.

It is likely to prove difficult in Wales – and probably also in the UK as a whole – to protect post-16 education and training from such cuts. This will reinforce the importance of collaboration between government and stakeholders to ensure a consensus on how best to deploy the public funding that is available. In those circumstances, it will be interesting to see whether the core values that underpin the political stability in Wales will crumble, or conversely, will be the bedrock on which education and training policy and delivery for the leaner times ahead will be based.

Summary and conclusions

Much of the description and analysis in the preceding sections of this chapter serves to support the thesis that devolution of powers has been accompanied by increasing divergence in policy frameworks, in governance and institutional arrangements, and in educational and training programmes in the separate parts of the UK. In part this can be seen as a result of the different political make-up of devolved governments compared with that of the UK government; in part it reflects different historical traditions and cultures that underlie the respective education and training systems, to which devolution has now afforded greater scope in influencing policy development; and to an extent it has resulted from the differing conclusions as to what policy approaches are best suited to the economic and social circumstances of the separate countries. Underlying these drivers towards divergence has been an expectation that devolution will in itself lead to the pursuit of distinctive policies and approaches in each part of the UK.

However, the analysis suggests that it is not simply a matter of Scotland, Wales and Northern Ireland diverging from an established Westminster-led system dominated by a predominantly English perspective. Arguably, there has been a greater degree of turbulence and change in the English education and training system since 1997 than in those in other parts of the UK. This has manifested itself in five reallocations of responsibilities between government departments, involving a total of seven differently named departments. There have been three separate systems for planning and funding of post-16 education and training, each involving complex and essentially top-down arrangements for translating government policy into local delivery through national, local and (to a lesser degree) regional and sub-regional agencies.

The latest arrangements, which only came into force in 2010, seem unlikely to survive under a new administration committed to abolishing quangos and devolving more responsibility to the local level. The qualifications and curriculum framework and the national qualifications taken by young people have been under almost continuous review since 1997. This has again resulted in a succession of reforms and adaptations, with the stated aims of protecting standards (mainly of established general qualifications, particularly GCE A Levels), raising achievement levels and providing the range of pathways and opportunities required to meet the needs of the full 14–19 cohort. Finally, at the institutional level, the thrust of government policy – notwithstanding some initiatives aimed at encouraging greater collaboration – has in practice provoked a more competitive market involving an increasingly diverse range of providers and with great variations in the make-up of the provider network in different parts of the country.

Against this background, Scotland, Wales and Northern Ireland would have diverged from the English model even if they had merely continued to operate within the policies and governance arrangements that pre-dated devolution. However, as this chapter has shown, Scotland and Wales have sought to use their devolved powers to adapt their respective education and training systems to reflect their particular political priorities and circumstances and their own views of the education state. In many respects this has exacerbated the degree of divergence, as is perhaps most evident in three areas.

First, governance arrangements in Scotland and Wales now appear much more inclusive than those in England. The two countries have achieved this in different ways – Scotland predominantly through the close engagement of stakeholders and providers in the 'policy dialogue' and Wales through the abolition of quangos, which has necessitated a more direct relationship between the central department and providers. However, the effect in both cases has been to give those responsible for the delivery of education and training at local level a stronger sense of involvement in decisions affecting them. Seen through the eyes of their counterparts, the trend in England has, if anything, been in the opposite direction: an increased emphasis on a top-down approach to policy development and delivery, underpinned by the use of targets, funding levers and inspection regimes to monitor performance. The inclusiveness of the Scottish and Welsh approaches can in part be attributed to their smaller sizes (both can be seen in this respect as broadly equivalent to an English region). This undoubtedly makes it easier in practical and logistical terms to engage local authorities and provider networks. However, it also appears to derive from a more deeply rooted sense of social partnership in these countries than exists in England.

Second, whilst competition between institutions has gained momentum in England, collaboration remains the dominant ethos in Scotland and Wales. The active promotion of new institutions, often in direct competition with existing providers, has been resisted in the latter countries, both of which have retained much more homogeneous systems for the delivery of post-compulsory education and lifelong learning. This was already true prior to devolution and is more evidently the case now. Scotland's Colleges continue to play the leading role in Scotland, supported by a network of private training providers handling elements of vocational and specialist learning, but with little evidence of competition between them. In Wales, current policy is to move towards a smaller number of FE and sixth form providers, offering choice and diversity within – rather than between – institutions, and brought about very much through a spirit of collaboration and integration.

Third, the underlying rationale for skills policy has become much more distinctive in the different parts of the UK and this in turn has prompted more divergent approaches. Prior to devolution there was something of a consensus around the notion that the UK needed to increase the skills of its workforce in order to compete in the global economy and that qualifications could be seen as a proxy for skills.

While the emphasis on skills development remains an important policy driver in all parts of the UK, Scotland and Wales are now tailoring both the policy itself and the funding of specific skills programmes much more closely to their economic and social circumstances. This was perhaps most starkly demonstrated by the rejection in Scotland and Wales of the thrust of the Leitch Report (Leitch, 2006), which was seen as projecting an analysis predominantly reflecting the economic circumstances of the South East of England. It has also been reflected in major policy documents, *Skills for Scotland* (Scottish Government, 2007) and *Skills that Work for Wales* (DCELLS, 2008a), both of which arguably adopt a relatively more balanced approach in addressing demand- and supply-side factors affecting the supply of skills than the essentially supply-side emphasis of skills policy in England. Scotland has also been distinctive in emphasising the importance of skills utilisation rather than skills supply.

Northern Ireland, too, is reviewing its skills policy in the light of recent changes, not least the more stringent economic climate. The Department for Employment and Learning published a consultation document in June 2010 setting out proposals to update the earlier skills strategy and its associated implementation plan (DEL, 2010). This document places a heavy emphasis on the importance of skills in supporting a dynamic and innovative economy, echoing the themes of similar documents produced by the UK government in recent years. However, as with Scotland and Wales, there are clear indications of attempts to tailor the strategy and the proposed actions to the specific circumstances facing the Northern Ireland economy.

Of course, similarities remain in these diverging systems. In all parts of the UK the general, or academic, route still represents the pre-eminent means of progression to higher education for young people. Although the names of the programmes may differ, the funding priorities for post-16 learning and state-supported skills training have much in common. Qualification frameworks are somewhat similar throughout the UK, notwithstanding some differences in the names and nature of individual awards within these frameworks. A new Qualifications and Credit Framework is due to take effect from December 2010, providing the only recognised and regulated framework for vocational qualifications in England, Wales and Northern Ireland. Funding constraints arising from the current economic circumstances are likely to limit the scope for further divergence to the extent that all administrations in the UK will need to concentrate scarce resources on statutory and other 'core' provision, where priorities will often be similar. But as subsequent chapters will show, political forces for divergence will remain strong.

References

Ball, S. J. (1990) *Politics and Policymaking in Education: Explorations in policy sociology*. London: Routledge.

-- (2007) *Education Plc: Private sector participation in public sector education*. London: Routledge.

Coffield, F., Edward, S., Finlay, I., Hodgson, A., Spours, K. and Steer, R. (2008) *Improving Learning, Skills and Inclusion: The impact of policy on post-compulsory education*. London: Routledge.

Department for Business, Innovation and Skills (BIS) (2009) *Skills Investment Strategy*. London: BIS.

Department for Children, Education, Lifelong Learning and Skills (DCELLS) (2008a) *Skills that Work for Wales: A skills and employment strategy and action plan*. Cardiff: WAG.

-- (2008b) *Transforming Education and Training Provision in Wales: Delivering skills that work for Wales*. Cardiff: WAG.

-- (2009) *For Our Future: The 21st century higher education strategy and plan for Wales*. Cardiff: WAG.

-- (2010) *Welsh-medium Education Strategy*. Cardiff: WAG.

Department for Children, Schools and Families (DCSF) (2008) *Participation in Education, Training and Employment by 16–18 Year Olds in England*. Statistical First Release 13/2008. London: DCSF.

Department for Education and Employment (DfEE) (2000) *Remit Letter from the Secretary of State to the Learning and Skills Council*. London: DFEE. <http://readingroom.lsc.gov.uk/pre2005/about/purpose/lsc-remit-letter.pdf> (accessed 19 October 2010).

Department for Education and Skills (DfES) (2004) *Five Year Strategy for Children and Learners*. London: DfES.

Department for Employment and Learning (DEL) (2010) *Success through Skills 2: The skills strategy for Northern Ireland*. Belfast: DEL.

Department for the Economy and Transport (DE&T) (2010) *Economic Renewal: A new direction*. Cardiff: Welsh Assembly Government (WAG).

Gallacher, J. (2009) 'Higher education in Scotland's colleges: A distinctive tradition?'. *Higher Education Quarterly*, 63(4), 384–401.

Gallacher, J., Ingram, R. and Reeve, F. (2009) *Work-based and Work-related Learning in Higher National Certificates and Diplomas in Scotland and Foundation*

Degrees in England: A comparative study. Glasgow: Centre for Research in Lifelong Learning, Glasgow Caledonian University.

Hansard (2009) House of Commons Official Report, 21 July 2009, column 1504W.

-- (2010) Minutes of evidence taken before the Children, Schools and Families Committee, 8 March.

Hodgson, A. and Spours, K. (2006) 'An analytical framework for policy engagement: The contested case of 14–19 reform in England'. *Journal of Education Policy*, 21(6), 679–96.

House of Commons (2009) *Adult Education*. House of Commons Library Standard Note SN/SP/4941, 21 January. <www.parliament.uk> (accessed 12 October 2010).

Ingram, R., Mehdizadeh, N. and Gallacher, J. (2009) *Destination Study of Students Who Complete HNC/Ds*. Interim Report. Glasgow: Centre for Research in Lifelong Learning, Glasgow Caledonian University.

Learning and Skills Council (LSC) (2007) *The 16–18, Adult Learner- and Employer-responsive Funding Models*. Coventry: LSC.

-- (2008) *Government Investment Strategy 2009–10, LSC Grant Letter and LSC Statement of Priorities*. Coventry: LSC.

-- (2010) *Joint Advisory Committee for Qualifications Approval 2009 Biennial Review Report*. Coventry: LSC.

Leitch, S. (2006) *Prosperity for All in the Global Economy: World class skills*. London: HM Treasury.

National Assembly for Wales (2001) *The Learning Country: A paving document*. Cardiff: National Assembly for Wales.

-- (2005) *Wales: A Vibrant Economy*. Cardiff: National Assembly for Wales.

-- (2009) *Learning and Skills (Wales) Measure 2009*. Cardiff: The Stationery Office.

-- (2010a) *The Review of Further Education Governance in Wales*. Cardiff: National Assembly for Wales. <http://www.assemblywales.org/bus-home/bus-guide-docs-pub/bus-business-documents/bus-business-documents-written-min-state.htm?act=dis&id=194743&ds=6/2010> (accessed 14 August 2010).

-- (2010b) *The Review of Higher Education Governance in Wales*. Cardiff: National Assembly for Wales. <http://www.assemblywales.org/bus-home/bus-guide-docs-pub/bus-business-documents/bus-business-documents-written-min-state.htm?act=dis&id=194741&ds=6/2010> (accessed 14 August 2010).

New York Times (2009) 'In saving jobs, mixed efforts in EU'. *New York Times*. <http://www.nytimes.com/2009/10/23/business/global/23rglobaleur.html?_r=1&scp=1&sq=Proact&st=nyt> (accessed 14 August 2010).

Osborne, M. and Turner, E. (2002) 'Private training providers in Scotland'. *Journal of Vocational Education and Training*, 54(2), 267–94.

Ozga, J. (2000) *Policy Research in Education Settings: Contested terrain*. Buckingham: Open University Press.

Parry, G. (2009) 'Higher education, further education and the English experiment'. *Higher Education Quarterly*, 63(4), 322–42.

Raffe, D. (2007) 'Learning from "home international" comparisons: 14–19 policy across the United Kingdom'. In D. Raffe and K. Spours (eds), *Policy-making and Policy Learning in 14–19 Education*. London: Institute of Education, University of London.

Raffe, D. and Spours, K. (eds) (2007) *Policy-making and Policy Learning in 14–19 Education*. London: Institute of Education, University of London.

Raffe, D., Gallacher, J. and Toman, N. (2008) 'The Scottish Credit and Qualifications Framework: Lessons for the European Qualifications Framework'. *European Journal of Vocational Training*, 42, 59–69.

Scottish Executive (2005) *Lifelong Learning Partners: Scotland's schools and colleges building the foundation of a lifelong learning society: A guide to schools, colleges and local authorities*. Edinburgh: Scottish Executive.

Scottish Funding Council (SFC) (2009) *Corporate Plan 2009–12*. Edinburgh: Scottish Funding Council.

-- (2010a) *Learning for All: Fourth update on measures of success*. Edinburgh: Scottish Funding Council.

-- (2010b) *Infact Database*. Edinburgh: Scottish Funding Council, available online at <https://stats.sfc.ac.uk/infact/> (accessed 19 October 2010).

Scottish Government (2010) *Students in Higher Education at Scottish Institutions 2008–09*. Edinburgh: Scottish Government.

Scottish Parliament (2002) *Enterprise and Lifelong Learning Committee: 9th Report. Final Report on Lifelong Learning*. SP Paper 679. Edinburgh: The Stationery Office.

Skills Development Scotland (SDS) (2010) *National Training Programme Statistics*. <http://www.skillsdevelopmentscotland.co.uk/knowledge/reports/national-training-programmes-statistics.aspx> (accessed 15 September 2010).

Statistical Directorate (2009a) *Schools in Wales: General statistics 2009*. Cardiff: WAG. <http://wales.gov.uk/docs/statistics/2010/100629sdr982010v3en.pdf> (accessed 14 August 2010).

-- (2009b) *Further Education, Work-based Learning and Community Learning in Wales 2007/8*. Cardiff: WAG. <http://wales.gov.uk/docs/statistics/2009/091217 sdr2052009en.pdf> (accessed 14 August 2010).

-- (2010) *Further Education, Work-based Learning and Community Learning, 2008/09 and 2009/10 (early figures)*. Cardiff: WAG. <http://wales.gov.uk/topics/statistics/headlines/post16education2010/100422/?lang=en> (accessed 14 August 2010).

UK Parliament (1988) *Education Reform Act*. London: UK Parliament.

-- (1992) *Further and Higher Education Act*. London: UK Parliament.

Wales Employment and Skills Board (WESB) (2010) *Moving Forward: Foundations for growth*. Cardiff: WESB.

Webb Review (2007) *Promise and Performance: The report of the independent review of the mission and purpose of further education in Wales*. Cardiff: WAG.

Welsh Assembly Government (WAG) (2007) *One Wales: A progressive agenda for the government of Wales*. Cardiff: WAG.

Working Group on 14–19 Reform (2004) *Final Report of the Working Group on 14–19 Reform*. London: DfES.

Chapter 6

Policy into practice:
Provider perspectives

David James

Introduction

Building on the fourth seminar in the 'New Directions' series, this chapter presents an account of the consequences of policy processes and structures for providers, at the level of colleges. The fundamental question here is whether (and if so to what extent) the sorts of differences that are discussed elsewhere in the book actually have an impact on practices. Do contrasting directions in policy leave practices largely untouched? Do people carry on teaching and learning in the same old (or new) ways regardless of policy direction and emphasis? Although the seminar series did not include a thoroughgoing research design that would provide a definitive answer to such questions, it nevertheless allowed for some well-founded discussion. The chapter draws on three sources: first, on the contributions of seminar series participants, and in particular three senior college leaders based in England, Scotland and Wales respectively; second, on subsequent interviews with four senior college leaders also from across those three countries; third, on the recent Economic and Social Research Council (ESRC) Teaching and Learning Research Programme (TLRP) project *Transforming Learning Cultures in Further Education*, the only large-scale independent study of teaching and learning in the FE sector in the UK. This project was chosen because, although it was based only in England, it did investigate the relationship between policy and practice, and it offered an approach in which the 'presence' of policy and the outcomes of policy were rendered visible in everyday practices.

The chapter begins with a brief mention of some difficulties of making comparisons between the three countries. It then introduces some key points of similarity and difference in the relationship between colleges and policy processes in England, Scotland and Wales, with a particular focus on: contexts for collaboration; mission, voice and connectedness; and relationships to quality regimes. The discussion of the potential significance of these similarities and differences is taken forward via the concept of *learning culture*, because this suggests how elements of policy can never be safely relegated to 'mere context', but have to be understood for their impact on practices on the ground.

A difficult context for comparison

It would be a demanding enough task to compare experiences of policy development, implementation and consequences in three countries, even if the focus was narrowly upon 'policy affecting colleges of further education'. What complicates a comparison of England, Scotland and Wales is that they cannot be considered as separate entities. One must not only keep in the mind the shifting differences and overlaps in remit and statutory responsibility of Westminster, Edinburgh and Cardiff; but also the problem of a cultural tendency which often sees commentary on 'Britain' or 'the UK' giving enormous weight to English examples and where the position of Scotland and Wales is left ambiguous.

Let us begin with two recent examples of high-level policy ambition:

> *Moving from good to great public services can only be achieved by Whitehall letting go and empowering staff to shape local provision to meet local needs and priorities.*
>
> (Gordon Brown, 2009)

> *Our plans for decentralization are based on a simple human insight: if you give people more responsibility, they behave more responsibly... We will require the people and organisations acting for the state to be directly accountable to the people they are supposed to serve. They will have to stop treating them like children and start treating them like adults.*
>
> (David Cameron, 2009)

It can be safely assumed that both these statements were intended (and were largely taken) to pertain to 'Britain'. Yet in the case of further education at least, the problem they are aimed at tackling is much more of an English one than it is a Welsh or Scottish one. A college principal in England summed up the situation as follows:

> *Increasingly the context is one of a top-down, planning-led environment in which quangos determine not just the amount of money but precisely what qualifications and client groups are served and how much. It is a Kafkaesque scenario that would be unbelievable to most people outside FE. There are funding manuals, and books to*

interpret the funding manuals, lots of top down bureaucracy, armies of people employed to make sure you are complying with a particular interpretation of the rules.

(Principal of a large FE college in England, May 2010)

He went on to state that English FE has been a 'test bed' for a particularly rabid form of performativity, a point others have made a number of times (e.g. Hayes, 2003; Gleeson *et al.*, 2005; Coffield *et al.*, 2008) and which is further echoed in a series of recent studies exploring the ramifications of greater self-regulation (SR) in the learning and skills sector:

[R]espondents in the different sectors expressed similar concerns that their views were not being taken into account within current policy debates about SR. FE college Principals were frustrated that they were not included in these debates, and so too were many respondents in private training providers and in the adult and community learning sector.

(Collinson, 2009: 1)

There is a notable irony here, given that the topic was a form of autonomy. In one of the component reports exploring the voice of college leaders, the authors describe a 'strong consensus', with principals identifying a need for more devolution of responsibility to colleges. Regimes of regulation had become 'dysfunctional' and increased devolution was seen as 'allowing colleges to respond flexibly and creatively to the needs of their communities' (Chapman *et al.*, 2009: 9). The report goes on to comment:

This top-down, managerialist approach is now being questioned both within government and by authoritative external commentators (e.g. the Foster Review 2005). Whilst the tightly managed regime since 1997 could be seen to have improved quality, increased...responsiveness and reduced poor provision, it is increasingly viewed as breeding micro management, excessive control from the centre, a rigid 'soviet tractor mentality' and a compliance culture, all of which has damaging consequences. The government accepts that the next great leap in public services from 'good to great' will require innovation, flexibility and ownership from front line staff. There is a growing recognition that this leap requires each college to have greater autonomy to meet the needs of its locality, flexibly and creatively.

(Chapman *et al.*, 2009: 9)

This diagnosis is a helpful starting point for asking whether the relationships colleges have to policy appear different in Scotland and Wales, and then whether or not this is likely to matter, and to whom.

Contexts for collaboration

As was noted in Chapter 1, the neo-liberal reforms associated with Thatcherism, so highly visible in England from the early 1980s, were to some extent resisted in Scotland and Wales, and the subsequent processes of devolution have built upon these differences. These underlying cultural issues and the varying influence of neo-liberal thinking are a suitable point at which to begin a comparison.

In Wales, momentous economic changes (especially in the valleys of the south and in respect of mining and the steel industry) give a distinctive context for contemporary FE provision. The most visible effect is high unemployment. However, policy affecting FE provision is also generated and interpreted against a backdrop of a high prevalence of socialist values and cooperative endeavour. It is likely that this history has contributed to the forging of genuinely collaborative arrangements of the sort (increasingly) necessary to be successful in bidding for European or regeneration grant money. There is also direct promotion of collaboration from the Welsh Assembly. As one college leader said:

> First of all I would compare it to England…competition there is pretty sharp, because the funding mechanism requires it, and it is a very Thatcherite funding mechanism. Wales has a different tradition, coming from the industrial revolution and from socialism, of trying to work together more. We have more cooperatives, we actually have a body in the Welsh Assembly that seeks to increase the number of cooperatives, and to make them much more effective. So there is an underlying feeling that in the public sector at the very least, bodies should work together. The Assembly has said that right from the beginning…they don't necessarily see that as putting colleges back into local authority control…but they do seek to find ways to enable schools and colleges to work together, colleges and colleges to work together, universities and colleges to work together more effectively. The first few years they had the policy but they were not particularly good at it, so it was more hectoring than reality. But things like the European Union funding, that Wales has had quite a lot of, Objective One, and now the latest round, have meant that to get the funds, bodies had to work together. At first it was 'well alright, we'll sign the letter of intent for each other, and you'll get yours and I'll get mine', but it has moved beyond that, certainly with the latest round, where the Welsh Assembly has been looking for much larger and broader projects, and therefore lip service partnership is no longer good enough…So in reality, you are obliged to work together. So there is some real pressure, mainly driven out of Europe, but then it spills across to other things.
>
> (College Principal, Wales)

This principal went on to describe how these tendencies also had to be understood in the context of Wales as a small country, which if it were part of England would perhaps be one or two counties. It has a population under three million, yet has regions, and 22 local authorities, a feature that could often frustrate efforts to achieve social change and one that was sometimes described as 'Redwood's revenge'.[1]

A particularly influential policy in Wales is focused on 'transformation' (DCELLS, 2008). This major policy document is about bringing together schools, colleges, work-based learners and higher education to find more efficient and effective ways of organising provision. Part of its executive summary gives a strong sense of its texture as a policy:

> This paper proposes a national framework to support the transformation of the provider network in Wales and invites proposals to be submitted that respond to the need for change. We have very deliberately designed the national transformation framework to encourage local solutions to local needs, rather than apply a one-size-fits-all model across Wales. The framework also recognizes that discussions between providers on new ways of working together are already happening around Wales – we warmly welcome these initiatives.
>
> (DCELLS, 2008: 5)

There have been more successful and less successful examples of such transformations to date, but one of the more successful was where a local authority and a university had agreed to build a new sixth form college on a site next to an existing FE college, which the FE college would run. Instead of having four secondary schools, each trying to provide a sixth form, there would now be a large provider that could offer a much better range of opportunities. Although it had taken many years to come to fruition, this example had itself been important for policy. It had 'inspired the transformation agenda in Wales':

> When you look across Wales, far too many of the sixth forms are small, and the Welsh averages for UCAS points and numbers going on to higher education are well below those for England...people don't get a good deal from the sixth forms, though there are some exceptions. But especially in the valleys, I think education would be improved by removing sixth forms throughout the valleys area.
>
> **Interviewer:** Are you facing new encouragements at the moment for new forms of collaboration or partnership?
>
> Yes, we have what's called the Learning and Skills Measure [National Assembly for Wales, 2009]. That says that at the age of 14, schools

have to offer 28 courses, of which at least six have to be vocational, and they can't offer them without working with a college for work-based learning...And at 16 they've got to provide 32 (courses), again with at least six being vocational. The Assembly has made it clear to schools that it will be reviewing not only what they offer, but what people actually do.

Interviewer: *And mergers?*

We are seeing six mergers between colleges going on...We are regularly spoken to by the Assembly. They have set a size, they say if you have a budget of £15 million you're viable, but equally it would be nice if there were fewer colleges. So the encouragement is not that powerful....In Powys, there is a different model...a 'distributed sixth form' to overcome the geographical challenges.

(College Principal, Wales)

In Scotland there is what one college leader described as a 'high level of dialogue between colleges and the central administration'. There is frequent and extensive collaboration, not only within the FE sector but between colleges and community groups, various sector bodies and local authorities (and to a lesser extent between colleges and schools). In England, collaboration is of course present, but as described by the Nuffield Review of 14–19 Education and Training, the system is essentially 'divided (in both curricular and institutional terms), competitive, and weakly collaborative' (Hayward *et al.*, 2005: 172). This is, as the Review also points out, to do with policy that simultaneously drives competition and cooperation. It is also, however, to do with questions of scale and how colleges and college leaders are positioned within each of the three systems.

Interviews with college leaders suggest strongly that in Wales and Scotland, providers are closer to policy and policy-makers than they are in England. This is first an issue of scale – Wales has 21 colleges, Scotland has 43, whilst England has 361. However, and linked to scale, it is also to do with organisation. Colleges in Wales work together through *ColegauCymru*,[2] and those in Scotland through *Scotland's Colleges*,[3] sharing a voice and to some extent, presenting a united front in policy processes. In England, the *Association of Colleges* (AOC)[4] is a large organisation with a national and regional structure. A further grouping, the *157 Group*[5] was established in March 2006: this group currently represents 28 large and mainly urban colleges.[6] A comparison of the websites of the four bodies suggests that the 157 Group has a particularly clearly articulated and distinctive mission, and its ambitions have more in common with the Scottish and Welsh bodies than with the larger, mainly English, Association of Colleges.

A further contrast is to be found in the greater number of agencies with an interest or remit bearing upon the English learning and skills sector encompassing further education colleges (see Chapter 5 for a discussion of these).

Mission, voice and connectedness

Yet differences seem to rest on more than scale, provider organisations and proximity to policy-makers. This became particularly clear in comparing the accounts of the college leaders when they spoke about the mission of their college. It is easy to be cynical about mission statements, but we can say that they are an expression of the direction, purpose and ambitions of the organisation and are generally the result of a process that encapsulates the collective wishes of a governing body. For this reason they are an important yardstick, and all the college leaders interviewed referred to college mission in explaining their grounds for optimism or pessimism at the current time.

In Scotland, a specific college mission to listen hard and respond to emerging needs in the community had meant that college tutors and leaders were often the first people to notice subtle clues in the local or regional economy: these would include shifts in skill requirements or changes in patterns of employment or in economic migration. On several occasions, an increase or decrease in enquiries from different sorts of learner had functioned as an early warning of something requiring a policy-level response (examples were a decline in certain kinds of apprenticeship in marine engineering and an increase in asylum-seekers and refugees seeking to take advantage of provision for ESOL). After some degree of sharing between colleges, such messages could lead to – and *had* led to – shifts in policy and resource allocation. Here, we might conceive of colleges as being connected vertically and horizontally in a web-like structure, which is sensitive to vibrations that are quite distant from the centre. College missions are important in this process – part of the remit and mandate to college leaders to share information and act on behalf of the college – and there is some confidence that the messages that are 'passed up the chain' can produce system-level readjustments.

There is a telling comparison to be made here with an English example. One college leader described how new funding rules, coupled with a substantial reduction in resources, would mean a large number of redundancies among staff. However, it also meant that the college's long-standing commitments to parts of the community were now in serious jeopardy. The example is particularly revealing of the status of college mission and the nature of the connections with policy-making:

Our adult contract is being cut. And it isn't even just a cut, it's that LSC [Learning and Skills Council] is saying, 'we want you to deliver this, this and this'. We are having to come out of what the LSC says is no longer a priority. Now much of that is community work, engagement work, low level – some of it not even Basic Skills...And the LSC is now saying, 'our priority has to be this shape, and that's what you've got to do'. So we are now having to come out of things that [the local authority] and the local community would want us to do, and do things that are fundable. Those priorities are national; now you could say that's fine, they are national priorities, but as a college, our mission is not to meet national priorities. Our college mission is to meet the needs of [the local area]. But the mission is becoming almost irrelevant.

Interviewer: *Are there particular casualties of that? Who are they?*

Yes. The whole Somalian community is a casualty, because there is no way we can put any funding for ESOL that is not accredited ESOL. But many in the Somalian community are illiterate in their own language, so they can't access accredited ESOL. We do work in other areas around courses that are trying to get people back into learning, 'first steps' courses. That sort of work will be more difficult to gain funding for. It is ridiculous. Teaching assistants are no longer fundable unless they're NVQ.[7] Now we have a very successful course for people who want to become Teaching Assistants. We will have to offer it as a full-cost course, so only certain people can afford it, and the people doing it are often unemployed and they can't afford it. Part-time A levels we will no longer be able to offer, they [students] will have to do it full time or pay full cost. Counselling courses we won't be able to offer any more. And some of the reasons they are not priority is that the actual qualification for a technical reason doesn't sit on the QCF [Qualifications and Credit Framework][8]... so it's not even that someone has <u>decided</u> that Counselling is not a priority. And there's also the international qualification for people who want to be mechanics on aircraft – it's a qualification they have to have. We are one of the few places providing it, but it is no longer fundable.

(Vice-Principal, England)

The college in which this senior figure is based is large and very well established. Yet it is important to note that compared to both the Welsh and Scottish examples, there appeared to be a completely different set of relationships framing communications between colleges and the making and implementation of policy. Where the college leaders in Wales and Scotland felt (and readily illustrated) their connectedness to policy-makers, in England it was more a case of a default disconnectedness: first, between colleges and policy-makers, and second, between policy-makers and an 'arm's length' funding agency. This disconnectedness required special effort and resources in order to overcome it. Recognising this, the governors in one college had consciously appointed a new Principal who would be a political player:

> **Interviewer:** *So how much of a say do you get? Who listens? Who do you talk to?*
>
> *...the Principal is trying to address this now. He's in London almost daily, trying to address these problems, attending Select Committees, talking to ministers. But whether they can change anything now is another question. It is probably quite an interesting case study, the way we are trying to work. At local level, at the LSC, there is really nobody you can have a conversation with about this. And this is not a criticism of the individuals, it's the way the system works. It's 'this is national policy, the computer calculates this'. And there's no-one we can have a conversation with regionally about this either.*
>
> **Interviewer:** *It's like an algorithm, isn't it?*
>
> *Yes...so the only people [the Principal] can have a conversation with is nationally...or [by] talking to the local authority, the leader of the council, because what's happening will have a big impact on them, so [we are] trying to use them for lobbying. We are working with MPs... we held a stakeholders' meeting, we invited all the MPs, anybody really, who might be able to bring some pressure.*
>
> (College Governor, England)

Relationships to quality regimes

The accounts of college leaders from England, Scotland and Wales also suggested some subtle but important differences in the nature of college engagement with inspection and related quality processes. One college principal (with experience of both systems) compared Wales and England in the following manner:

> *We have an inspectorate called Estyn and there is a framework that is very similar to England. But England, certainly for the last 10 or 15 years, has had an inquisitorial system. It's quite harsh, actually. It's holding you up to the light, you're not performing, so we'll pillory you. The Welsh system has leanings like that, but it is actually quite a bit more supportive, and it will listen to people more...Over the last two years, all the colleges in Wales have had improving grades, and we are heralded by the Inspectorate as the successful part of the education system.*

Interviewer: So are there elements of the old HMI 'professional' approach?

Yes, and spreading good practice, yes there is. And also we have a body like the AoC, called ColegauCymru, and through that, we do a lot of sharing of good practice, a lot, far more than you would see in England.

Interviewer: So is it just college principals who get together for that?

No, no, it's heads of department, heads of section. For example we have an annual conference for the business studies teachers. HR [Human Resources] people get together, finance people too. There are something like 43 networks for sharing good practice, and I would say about 30 of those are curriculum areas, so that makes quite a difference. And we do talk to the Inspectorate and to the Assembly about what they mean by quality, and do they know what they mean by quality.

Interviewer: So you do function as a pressure group.

Yes, as a lobby group. And we are exploring at the moment self-regulation. One of the tasks for this year is to come up with a model for self-regulation for colleges.

(College Principal, Wales)

This account illustrates the point made earlier about organisations. It also indicates a positive regard for (and a positive engagement with) a quality regime. What is perhaps most interesting about it is that it came from a principal who had had a very negative experience just a few years earlier, in which an inspection process had presented an account of a college that he, the staff and the governors found 'unrecognizable'. Subsequently the college had 'stood its ground', questioning the conduct of the inspection and the legitimacy of the outcome.

In Scotland, a recent review of inspection had included college leaders and had powerfully reinforced the idea that quality assurance was a collective responsibility:

I think [that here] it is different to England. We worked with the Inspectorate and the Funding Council to conduct a review of the inspection model that we had, and it is a review model that we have now...We used to have an inspection framework which suggested what you had to have, whereas now it's up to us to determine, by evidence, what should be included. We have Her Majesty's Inspectorate (HMI) as the one agency that looks right across education, and they have now taken on looking at provision outwith colleges, in a wider way. So we share Her Majesty's Inspectors with the schools, community learning and development, but now also with Jobcentre Plus, and prisons. In any inspection you would have a lead officer, but in my college I'll have a number of people who are associate inspectors, who work for the inspector, and I will agree to their release...and they go away for a week to do an inspection and then they come back. Every college in Scotland has some associates in it. In the beginning they were concentrated in a small number of colleges. But everyone started to see that associates were helping to develop a greater understanding, so it was a positive thing. Those are selected by HMI, and on the panel there would also be a principal.

(College Principal, Scotland)

In England, there is a widely held perception that the inspection regime is moving back towards a model that includes greater dialogue. A recent inspection of part of the provision of a large college had endorsed all the strengths and areas for improvement identified in the college's own self-assessment and provided one further issue which had not been identified by the college itself. Carried out under a revised approach, introduced from September 2009, the inspection was the first the college had had which made *recommendations* as well as giving grades (in the past, inspections would provide 'areas for improvement'). Colleges in general welcomed and valued this shift, since it opened up the possibility of a conversation or a dialogue about the different ways in which a recommendation could be responded to. One college leader also pointed out the advantages of only having a few weeks of notice of an inspection, and though this did mean that 'we did nothing else for four weeks', dealing with inspection was at least limited to that period.

College leaders at the college being inspected were content with the outcome of the inspection, and pleased that the inspection had been characterised by more dialogue than some in the past. It had also been 'very capably led by someone who understood what the college was about'. At the same time, various college personnel were critical of how inspectors seemed to make assumptions on not very much evidence. The college leader in question said, 'I do have an issue with the level of observations. They do 50, and make an assumption, and we do 900'. Inspectors had also formed impressions on the basis of single, unrepresentative incidents, and college staff were irritated that they had to put considerable energy into demonstrating that such impressions were unfounded.

These revised arrangements for inspection are perceived by many in the sector as representing a more proportionate and efficient use of Ofsted resources, as well as giving a more thoroughgoing role to self-assessment. However, college leaders at the college being inspected felt a heavy irony in all this. No sooner had the college been judged to be outstanding in meeting learner needs and in partnerships (both were central to the college mission) than it now faced the effects, described earlier, of remote and formulaic funding decisions which undermined its very strengths. It would seem that a clear and collective mission *and* independent evidence that the associated practices are 'outstanding', can still add up to little in terms of influence on policy.

Learning cultures

It is one thing to draw the sorts of comparisons made thus far, and to try to learn from them. Yet how important are they? Is it possible (as was suggested in one of the seminar discussions preceding this book) that similarities and differences of the order we have been identifying may not actually matter much to learners and teachers, those 'on the ground' in colleges? To address this point, we turn here to the concept of *learning cultures*. Developed within the ESRC TLRP, in the project *Transforming Learning Cultures in Further Education* ('the TLC project'), the concept challenges the idea that teaching and learning are just individual activities that happen to be located in an institutional, geographical, political or economic setting.

The argument is that teaching and learning are much better understood as *practices* that are part of a *learning culture*. The original project, which focused on FE in England, proposed that a great deal of what happens in the name of learning is highly structured by systems and mechanisms of inspection, funding and audit as well as the nature of the relationship to a vocational field, or to other vocational and academic programmes. Of course, tutors, managers and students do a great deal to reshape these effects in various ways, and are themselves important contributors to the learning culture in accordance with their dispositions, values or pedagogic preferences. The central point here is that these people are 'representing' (as well as 're-presenting') something: they embody and enact the structures around them, but not exactly as they please. Furthermore, this matters greatly because:

> *A learning culture will permit, promote, inhibit or rule out certain kinds of learning. This means that the key issue is how different learning cultures enable or disable different learning possibilities for the people that come into contact with them.*
>
> (James and Biesta, 2007: 28)

A learning culture is not, then, just another way of talking about the environment around the learner or the learning process, and as such it suggests a conscious break with the various psychological models that position learning as individualised and primarily cognitive. As the social practices through which people learn, a learning culture is a way of bringing into view (and keeping in view) the circumstances that have given us a current set of practices, and which current practices reproduce, refine or challenge. The concept is helpful on a variety of 'scales' too: just as a course of study has a learning culture, so might a college, a particular qualification, and to some extent an entire sector. This is another way of saying that any particular practice will be an expression of a set of forces (or a *field* in Bourdieu's sense – see e.g. Grenfell and James, 2004; Vandenberghe, 2000).

Zooming out: The learning culture of the FE sector

The TLC project suggested that one of the distinctive features of the English FE sector was the nature and source of policy concerned with teaching and learning and its improvement. The project noted a paradox: that repeated calls for the improvement of teaching and learning in FE were accompanied by a silence about learning. Coffield's earlier comment on this issue still seemed apposite:

> *In all the plans to put learners first, to invest in learning, to widen participation, to set targets, to develop skills, to open access, to raise standards, and to develop a national framework of qualifications, there is no mention of a theory (or theories) of learning to drive the whole project. It is as though there existed in the UK such a widespread understanding of, and agreement about, the processes of learning and teaching that comment was thought superfluous. The omission is serious, and, if not corrected, could prove fatal to the enterprise.*
> (Coffield, 2000: 18)

The TLC project argued that in some 50 years' worth of policy documents and related literature, there were continued appeals about the need to improve teaching and learning, but very little that addressed how this might actually be done. There were three main drivers in the policy 'stories' about required improvements. One was to do with the 'problems of youth and social cohesion'; another was 'the effectiveness of the provision', particularly in regard to the needs of employers or the need for particular skills; the last was the role of FE in the wider economy, often in the context of global competitiveness. At first glance this appeared to change in the White Paper *Further Education: Raising skills, improving life chances* (DfES, 2006), because it contained an explicit 'national strategy for teaching and learning in Further Education'. However, once again this did not discuss the nature of teaching and learning, concentrating instead on the agencies, frameworks and mechanisms which it was hoped would 'drive up quality'. The researchers concluded:

These largely indirect exhortations to improve teaching and learning therefore entail two conflicting assumptions, which we would argue continue to plague the sector. The first is that FE should provide effective responses – sometimes solutions – to a diverse array of social, industrial and economic needs. The second is that this should be achieved with ever-increasing efficiency. Pedagogy is little more than the 'pharmakos' here (Girard, 1977), the scapegoat paraded through these tales but then expelled from them.

(Colley *et al.*, 2007: 49)

The silence identified by Coffield above and then underlined by the TLC project is no doubt due in part to the sheer diversity of provision that is encompassed in FE colleges. This diversity is conventionally understood as a diversity of subjects, vocational areas and levels. The TLC analysis showed that a diversity of concepts and practices of teaching and learning was just as important. For example, one could find, side by side in the same college, a course where learning was defined mainly in terms of acquisition, and another in which it largely took the form of participation (see Sfard, 1998, for a helpful discussion of such metaphors). If we add to this the sector's celebrated flexibility and responsiveness to a diverse array of requirements and needs, we begin to see why it is that colleges appear more vulnerable to policy than schools and universities. Colleges 'embody' flexibility and responsiveness, and a plurality of legitimate practices, which are quite different but all called 'learning'. The Foster Review saw this as a major problem, arguing that 'above all, FE lacks a clearly recognized and shared core purpose'. It went on to reassert two of the regular 'policy stories' already mentioned, insisting that 'the way forward in resolving these causes [*sic*] includes an appetite to catch up with competitive international economies' and 'a consequential core focus on skills and employability' (Foster, 2005: 6).

Whether or not one agrees with the diagnosis and remedy presented by Foster, it is possible to argue that the embodying of diversity mentioned above means that FE learning cultures are *especially* prone to a high degree of policy prescription. If this is the case, the corollary is that colleges have little or no voice in policy processes and are forced constantly to respond to policy shifts with relatively little mediation or home-grown variation. The only way that colleges could change the key characteristics of this relationship is through organisation of the sort that has been much more evident in Wales and Scotland than in England (but which may be developing, for some, via the newer 157 Group in England).

Zooming in: Management and professionalism in the learning culture

The TLC project noted the affinity between, on the one hand, the 'entrepreneurial' nature of FE colleges, responding to constant changes in policy that affect the nature and volume of work and, on the other hand, staff recruitment practices characterised by informality and uncertainty. The frequent use of fractional and temporary contracts, a proliferation of roles and titles, and the lack of parity with other sectors of the educational world had all contributed towards casualisation and low morale. Against this backdrop, the researchers looked at what ideas about professionalism had currency 'on the ground'. A surprising finding here was that whilst many tutors complained about issues such as pay, regimes of audit and inspection, lack of recognition of their expertise, reduced autonomy through performance management and so on, these complaints did not seem to come from a shared or particular political position. Instead:

> *they arose from strong commitments to teaching, to fostering student learning and development, to attending to learners' needs, and to self-development of learning as a professional. Time and again, our data gave us examples of tutor frustration because regimes of funding, management and audit/inspection prevented or made more difficult the exercise of judgement based on experience.*
>
> (James and Gleeson, 2007: 130)

The real surprise here was the strength and depth of professional identity, meaning so much more than the 'restricted' idea of doing a job well in terms of a specification. Whilst the college leaders and managers continually responded to the shifting policy agenda in order to maintain the college as a business, tutors invariably had their own strongly-held positions on what was possible, reasonable or desirable in the circumstances. Sometimes this led to tutors resigning (as, for example, in the case of a modern languages A Level, where the class contact hours per week were reduced year on year until they reached a level the tutor regarded as unsustainable and incompatible with doing a worthwhile job). For others it led to 'underground learning', where a clash between systems and tutors' own values resulted in considerable self-imposed exploitation, as they strove to personally resource activity they regarded as still being necessary but which college resources no longer supported (see James and Diment, 2003). For yet others it produced considerable subversion or 'principled infidelity' (Wallace and Hoyle, 2005), as tutors found ways of keeping up quality by mitigating the worst effects of the expectations of inspection, rules derived from audit, or a particular management requirement.

The tension between the audit culture and professionalism is a much-discussed topic (see, for example, Biesta, 2004; Ball, 2005; Coffield *et al.*, 2008; Sennett, 2009). We found that such things as performativity and the use of targets for progression, retention and achievement were not just 'context', and not just something for the outward-facing senior managers to respond to. Rather, they changed the nature of the tutor–manager relationship and in turn affected what tutors and students did together in practice. Some would argue that in FE, leadership and management are being supplanted by managerialism (defined as the assumption that 'all aspects of organisational life can and should be controlled...that ambiguity can and should be radically reduced or eliminated' (Wallace and Hoyle, 2005: 9)). As we noted in the TLC project:

> There is a strong affinity between a belief in managerialism and a continuing tendency to see professionalism as old-fashioned, as self-serving and as incapable of a flexible response to client need – and therefore as the wrong place to look for the generation of improvement.
>
> (James and Gleeson, 2007: 134)

The project demonstrated that a strong sense of professionalism had not been obliterated by increasing prescription or by a high pace of radical change in provision. On the contrary, it seemed likely that the pace of change in colleges (and what some termed 'the culture of the now') may even have helped to bolster a strong sense of professional identity separate to identifications with, or loyalties to, the college. Nevertheless, there were constant and sometimes painful clashes between tutors' professional dispositions, often formed much earlier and in different conditions, and the subsequent expectations or requirements placed upon them in the college. In Bourdieusian terms, this may be conceived as a *habitus* with professional capital, which is progressively less recognised in the *field*, rather like landing in a foreign city and having the wrong currency. Indeed, the more one has of the wrong currency, the greater the sense of injustice or inconvenience one might experience.

Conclusion

The analysis here underlines many of the conclusions reached by Raffe and Spours (2007) in their comparison of models of policy learning and policy-making in 14–19 education. Some three years on, there seems to be continued evidence for their observation that Scotland and Wales can be characterised as a collaborative model, where, 'Many of the institutional forms associated with the politicized model in England, such as central policy units and non-elected advisers detached from policy departments, are absent or weaker' (20). They also noted 'a spirit of partnership [which] has informed policy development and implementation' (21).

As well as adding some confirmation to such distinctions, this discussion has pointed to quite sharp contrasts in the nature of the connections and relationships between providers and policy-makers and policy processes between the three countries. Of particular note is how college mission continues to have a saliency or legitimacy in Scotland and Wales which, it seems, may be being lost in England. There also appear to be marked differences in the policy-framed expectations and possibilities for collaboration with other colleges and between colleges and other providers. Furthermore, and most marked of all, there is at least some evidence in Scotland and Wales suggesting that dialogue with (and occasional influence upon) policy-makers is a normal expectation of all parties. By contrast, some leaders in English colleges perceive that they have little or no chance to influence the development and implementation of policy, and it would appear that even the most determined efforts of this kind may have little impact.

In preparing this chapter, it has not been possible to conduct a repeated TLC project for Scottish and Welsh FE and thereby provide equivalent data and analysis to the English case. Yet, for present purposes, this is not a significant problem. Though it was conducted in England, the TLC project is most useful here as a reminder that the texture of policy does reverberate right through to what teachers and learners and others actually do 'on the ground'. To put this another way, the nature and tone of the relationships between colleges and the individuals, agencies and policies that frame their work – something we have seen can differ markedly between England, Scotland and Wales – is one of the most important things shaping the learning culture. The recent denial of ESOL to large swathes of a Somalian community in an English city, with no discussion of whether that is what the college or any section of its community would see as the best way to realise a cut in resources, is just a particularly visible example of something that is ever-present.

Acknowledgements

I am very grateful to the college leaders who were so generous with their time. I would also like to thank Bryn Davies, Dennis Gunning, Ann Hodgson, Linda McTavish, Judith Stradling and Martyn Waring for their comments on an earlier draft.

Notes

1   John Redwood was Conservative Secretary of State for Wales between 1993 and 1995 in John Major's Cabinet.

2   See <http://www.colegaucymru.ac.uk/who_we_are-6.aspx> (accessed 15 October 2010).

3   See <http://www.scotlandscolleges.ac.uk/scotlands-colleges/about-us/about-us.html> (accessed 15 October 2010).

4   See <http://www.aoc.co.uk/en/about_us/> (accessed 15 October 2010).

5   See <http://www.157group.co.uk/welcome> (accessed 15 October 2010).

6   As at August 2010 – see <http://www.157group.co.uk/> (accessed 15 October 2010).

7   That is, unless the courses include a National Vocational Qualification.

8   The Qualifications and Credit Framework. See <http://www.qcda.gov.uk/qualifications/60.aspx> (accessed 15 October 2010).

References

Ball, S. J. (2005) 'Education reform as social barbarism: Economism and the end of authenticity'. The Scottish Educational Research Association Lecture 2004. *Scottish Educational Review*, 37(1), 4–16.

Biesta, G. J. J. (2004) 'Education, accountability and the ethical demand: Can the democratic potential of accountability be regained?'. *Educational Theory*, 54(3), 233–50.

Brown, G. (2009) *Working Together: Public services on your side*. Cabinet Office. Norwich: HMSO. <http://www.hmg.gov.uk/media/15556/workingtogether.pdf> (accessed 12 October 2010).

Cameron, D. (2009) 'The Big Society' Speech. <http://www.conservatives.com/News/Speeches/2009/11/David_Cameron_The_Big_Society.aspx> (accessed 9 September 2010).

Chapman, R., Collinson, D. and Collinson M. (2009) 'Giving voice to college leaders: The journey towards self-regulation?'. In D. Collinson (ed.), *Researching Self-Regulation in FE Colleges*. Coventry: Learning and Skills Improvement Service.

Coffield, F. (ed.) (2000) *Differing Visions of the Learning Society*, Vol. 1. Bristol: Policy Press.

Coffield, F., Edward, S., Finlay, I., Hodgson, A., Spours, K. and Steer, R. (2008) *Improving Learning, Skills and Inclusion: The impact of policy on post-compulsory education*. London: Routledge/Falmer.

Colley, H., Wahlberg, M. and James, D. (2007) 'Improving teaching and learning in FE: A policy history'. In D. James and G. J. J. Biesta (eds), *Improving Learning Cultures in Further Education*. London and New York: Routledge, 41–59.

Collinson, D. (ed.) (2009) *Researching Self-Regulation in FE Colleges*. Coventry: Learning and Skills Improvement Service.

Department for Children, Education, Lifelong Learning and Skills (DCELLS) (2008) *Transforming Education and Training Provision in Wales*. Welsh Assembly Government. <http://wales.gov.uk/docs/dcells/publications/100301transfor mationpolicyen.pdf> (accessed 8 September 2010).

Department for Education and Skills (DfES) (2006) *Further Education: Raising skills, improving life chances*. Department for Education and Skills Cm 6768. Norwich: The Stationery Office.

Foster, A. (2005) *Realising the Potential: A review of the future role of further education colleges*. Annesley: DfES Publications.

Gleeson, D., Davies, J. and Wheeler, E. (2005) 'On the making and taking of professionalism in the further education workplace'. *British Journal of Sociology of Education*, 26(4), 445–60.

Grenfell, M. and James, D. (2004) 'Change in the field: Changing the field. Bourdieu and the methodological practice of educational research'. *British Journal of Sociology of Education*, 25(4), 507–23.

Hayes, D. (2003) 'New labour, new professionalism'. In J. Satterthwaite, E. Atkinson and K. Gale (eds) *Discourse, Power and Resistance: Challenging the rhetoric of contemporary education*. Stoke on Trent: Trentham Books, 27–42.

Hayward, G., Hodgson, A., Johnson, J., Oancea, A., Pring, R., Spours, K., Wilde, S. and Wright, S. (2005) *Nuffield Review of 14–19 Education and Training, Annual Report 2004–05*. Oxford: University of Oxford Department of Educational Studies.

James, D. and Biesta, G.J.J. (2007) *Improving Learning Cultures in Further Education*. London: Routledge.

James, D. and Diment, K. (2003) 'Going underground? Learning and assessment in an ambiguous space'. *Journal of Vocational Education and Training*, 55(4), 407–22.

James, D. and Gleeson, D. (2007) 'Professionality in FE learning cultures'. In D. James and G. J. J. Biesta (eds), *Improving Learning Cultures in Further Education*. London: Routledge.

National Assembly for Wales (2009) *Learning and Skills (Wales) Measure (2009)*. <http://www.assemblywales.org/bus-home/bus-legislation/bus-leg-measures/business-legislation-measures-ls.htm> (accessed 8 September 2010).

Raffe, D. and Spours, K. (2007) 'Three models of policy learning and policy-making in 14–19 education'. In D. Raffe and K. Spours (eds), *Policy-making and Policy Learning in 14–19 Education*. London: Institute of Education, University of London.

Sennett, R. (2009) *The Craftsman*. London: Penguin Books.

Sfard, A. (1998) 'On two metaphors of learning and the dangers of choosing just one'. *Educational Researcher*, 27(2), 4–13.

Vandenberghe, F. (2000) '"The real is relational": An epistemological analysis of Pierre Bourdieu's generative structuralism'. In D. Robbins (ed.), *Pierre Bourdieu*, Vol. 2. London: Sage.

Wallace, M. and Hoyle, E. (2005) 'Towards effective management of a reformed teaching profession'. Paper for ESRC seminar series *Changing Teacher Roles, Identities and Professionalism*, King's College London. <http://www.kcl.ac.uk/content/1/c6/01/41/66/paper-wallace.pdf> (accessed July 2010).

PART 3

POSSIBLE FUTURE DIRECTIONS

Chapter 7

Convergence, divergence and post-devolution politics across the UK: The shaping role of the state, markets and democracy

Ken Spours

Introduction

This chapter explores the impact of the wider contexts of the state, markets and democracy in shaping reform options for public services and post-compulsory education and lifelong learning across the four countries of the UK. Earlier in the book the processes of 'convergence' and 'divergence' have been alluded to. Here they are explored more systematically as the relationship between the assemblies and parliaments of Scotland, Wales and Northern Ireland and the UK Westminster Government, arguably, reaches a new and unpredictable point following the May 2010 UK general election.

Bain (2010) asserts that the coherence of the British State, comprising the UK Westminster Government and its various apparatuses, is breaking up under the weight of parliamentary devolution. It will be suggested that processes of convergence and divergence in specific public services can be illuminated by this wider political analysis of state formation as new versions of state and civil society emerge in Scotland, Wales and Northern Ireland, albeit still within the shell of the UK state. This does not mean that the UK as a social and economic entity is breaking up, because the four countries, despite their asymmetry, are bound together in many ways. However, as Gareth Rees points out in Chapter 4, the political relationship between the three small countries and Westminster could now be placed under particular strain by proposed radical reductions in public expenditure. New conflicts may arise because these fundamental changes will be interpreted or mediated by emerging state and civil society configurations – the underlying histories and cultures, new political structures, accumulated differences in governance, policy-making and political perspectives – in the different countries. Following an analysis of these processes, the chapter will conclude with a brief discussion of 'post-devolution politics' and what this might mean for policy learning across the UK.

The state, markets and democracy: Some definitions

In this chapter the *state* is understood as the 'extended state'. Describing the development of the modern state in the period since 1870, the concept of the extended state embraces both governmental state and civil society. The 'governmental state' (e.g. central government and institutions such as the army, police and security services) on its own has been referred to as the minimalist or 'nightwatchman state' (Jessop, 1999). In addition and more recently, alongside and interacting with the governmental state has been a growing public sector and local government, together with elements of 'civil society', which includes a range of autonomous institutions such as registered charities, non-governmental organisations, community groups, women's organisations, faith-based organisations, professional associations, trades unions, self-help groups, social movements and business associations. The relationship between different sections of the state and civil society is complex, fluid and negotiated and, as we will see, politically contested.

Within the extended state lies a more specific 'education state' (Hodgson and Spours, 2006). The education state in the English case, for example, can be seen to comprise a range of national, regional and local structures and institutions, including the No. 10 Policy Unit, the Department for Education, regulatory and awarding bodies, inspectorates, funding bodies and public and private education providers. This definition, therefore, goes beyond purely governmental organisations and quangos and tries to capture the significant role of a set of key players within the contested landscape of education policy (Ball, 1990; Ozga, 2000). As with the more general definition of civil society, also included are education pressure groups, such as professional associations, teacher unions and think tanks, as well as the education media and key individuals, all of which exercise different degrees of political power and influence at different points in the policy process.

The term *markets* refers to the processes of marketisation of public services in which, for example, private providers displace public providers; public providers are converted to private providers (privatisation), public providers have to compete according to market drivers such as price and quality, and the public are seen as customers (Whitty and Power, 2000). Through these processes, marketisation and privatisation have, over the last 30 years, seen a general transfer of resources from the public to private sectors and these have been far more extensively deployed in England than in Scotland, Wales or Northern Ireland.

The concept of *democracy* is used here to refer to three aspects of governance and the degree to which the state and civil society operate democratically. At the national level, it refers to the degree of political legitimacy of national government and how far democratic systems represent the will of the people. Legitimacy, for example, can be increased by voting systems that reflect all shades of opinion (e.g. proportional representation) and by an executive that is held accountable by elected representatives. The second dimension of democracy is the relationship between national and other tiers of government. This can be enhanced by a significant role for local government because of its ability to understand the local environment and to reflect the needs of localities. The third dimension refers to the degree and character of popular participation in public life. This includes the role that communities and social partners play in shaping public services, the degree of openness of higher levels of government, how different social partners are involved in the accountability of different levels of government and how much autonomy they have to act within and beyond government itself.

Decentralisation and governance by network can reflect the development of democracy, but in themselves these processes cannot guarantee democratic life if, for example, they allow 'activist capture' (Newman and Clarke, 2009) or accentuate social differences between localities. The concepts of state, markets and democracy are not independent of one another; they always work in combination in different national and local contexts. At issue is the particular combination and which dimensions emerge as the most influential in shaping public services and options for reform in the different national contexts.

Convergence and divergence between national systems of the UK

Are we entering a new era?

The terms 'convergence' and 'divergence' in this book refer to the degree to which structures, policies and practices in post-compulsory education and lifelong learning are more common or different across the four countries of the UK (Raffe, 2005; Raffe *et al.*, 1999). Ozga (2005) suggests that divergence arises from the mediation or inflection of policy in 'local contexts' in an era of globalisation that has had the general effects of narrowing policy options. Here, it will be argued that the processes of policy translation in different national and state contexts can lead either to greater conformity and commonality across the different countries (convergence) or to degrees of difference (divergence), according to the ways in which particular state and civil society configurations are used to create and enact policy in the respective countries. The term 'divergence' is also used more specifically to refer to the mix of autonomous and reactive policy-making in Scotland, Wales and Northern Ireland in response to the policy agendas emanating from the sovereign UK Westminster Government (Raffe, 2009).

The end of the New Labour Government in 2010 and the election of a UK Conservative–Liberal Democrat Coalition Government has highlighted the powerful influence of political change. A new government committed to a neo-Thatcherite economic agenda will bring the relationship between Westminster and the assemblies and governments of the other countries into sharp relief. The period up until 1999 was one of administrative devolution for Scotland and Wales. Parliamentary devolution, the second and present era, built on what had gone before (Keating, 2005). Both periods saw a process of divergence, which was accelerated as new institutions were formed and more powers were devolved over the last decade. The new political situation, it will be argued, opens up a new period of uncertainty with regard to the relationship between the countries of the UK.

Underpinning this process of divergence is not only historic national identity, but growing political differences between England and Scotland and Wales. The two smaller nations have elected centre-left coalitions or minority governments and, as Chapters 3 and 4 point out, they have steered a broadly social democratic course on issues which have included: support for comprehensive schools and the role of local authorities; pay parity between school and further education sectors; and different policies on higher education tuition fees. England, on the other hand, has shown far more conservative tendencies. This includes not only the 1980s and Thatcherism, but the election of a centrist New Labour Government and its 'Third Way politics', with a language specifically created to win the support of 'middle England' (Fairclough, 2000). As, Ewart Keep points out in Chapter 2, in the area of post-compulsory education and lifelong learning, successive UK governments have adhered to fixed neo-liberal policy narratives on employment and skills which limit the horizons for policy-making in England particularly.

The suggestion of a possible 'new era' arises, however, from the observation of new fundamental forces at work; notably the election of a coalition government, headed by a Conservative Party rooted mainly in the South East of England, and the threat of a double-dip recession, fuelled by a public expenditure cuts agenda that will disproportionately affect those areas of the UK which have been historically dependent on the public sector.

Diverse views on divergence and the role of policy learning

Does the process of divergence matter? Viewed from a wider historical and political perspective the issue is hugely significant, but what is made of it depends on political perspective. Those who see the UK as an historic entity and support England's (or Westminster's) leading role may tolerate limited divergence in areas such as education so long as differences do not spread to the economy, foreign policy or defence and, in doing so, undermine the historical 'British State'. This has been the traditional position of the Conservative Party and it is difficult to imagine that, had it been in power at the end of the 1990s, parliamentary devolution would have been ceded. David Cameron now states that Conservative opposition to devolution post-1997 was a mistake and that 'we should have spent more time in government thinking – how do we give legitimate help to those people within our United Kingdom who want to have a greater expression of self-government?' (Cameron cited in Herald Scotland, 2009). There is an acceptance that this particular clock cannot be turned back and the new national settlements are part of the UK landscape. Not all Conservatives agree. Key political representatives in Wales, for example, view devolution as a slipway to 'socialism and separatism' (e.g. Crabb, 2007).

New Labour, on the other hand, supported devolution both from a social democratic perspective and as a means of heading off nationalist and separatist sentiment, particularly in Scotland. During the early days of the New Labour Government, the Labour Party was in the majority in England, Scotland and Wales and they had a great deal to lose in any disturbance of the emerging relationships. As Blair's recent biography demonstrates, the merits of Scottish devolution were debated within New Labour, with Blair himself declaring that 'I'm by temperament probably pretty unionist' (BBC, 2010a). Balanced against this was the fact that the Labour Party depended heavily on its Scottish and Welsh MPs in the House of Commons and failure to grant devolution would have fuelled support for the Scottish National Party (SNP) in its heartlands. Full Scottish and Welsh independence, on the other hand, would have reduced Westminster elections to England only, making it very difficult for the Labour Party to rule on its own in the foreseeable future. New Labour, therefore, invested a great deal in the relationship between Westminster and the other countries of the UK by attempting to meet Scottish demands for greater powers, but without breaking up the UK political system upon which it relied as a party. Its position on devolution was thus a delicate and pragmatic balancing act (Paterson, 2003).

Those to the left of New Labour may view divergence as an opportunity to seek alternatives to the dominant neo-liberal politics of the last 30 years. From Scottish and Welsh perspectives, this involves a recognition that their countries have held to a steady course of more social democratic policies and perspectives and resisted much of the English tide of Thatcherism in the 1980s and early 1990s (Holliday, 1992; Rees, 2004). These pre-Thatcherite and pre-New Labour positions were significantly strengthened by parliamentary devolution. Subsequent to this, the Welsh Labour Party declared 'clear red water' between itself and New Labour (Morgan, 2002) and the SNP in Scotland marked out a position broadly to the left of New Labour and, in doing so, succeeded in becoming a minority government in 2007. For reformers in England, on the other hand, the different policy trajectories being played out across the four countries provide opportunities for policy learning (Raffe and Spours, 2007; Jeffrey *et al.*, 2010). They can point to different policies on qualifications and curriculum, school organisation, higher education and tuition fees, and on teacher and lecturer pay being pursued in a UK context, in order to argue for similar policies to be put into practice in England. Policy learning is, therefore, a matter of political preference.

Given the political pragmatism that informed devolution from the English perspective, and the fact that England has been taking a different political trajectory to that of Scotland and Wales, there are few incentives currently in the established policy communities to engage in liaison, never mind policy learning. Trench (2009) observed that arrangements for liaison and coordination between governments have been under-developed, with a reliance on informal, *ad hoc* and bilateral liaison, and that the Plenary Joint Ministerial Committee, for example, which was supposed to convene annually to discuss key issues on the economy, health and poverty, did not meet at all between October 2002 and June 2008.

The dynamics of divergence and convergence: Emerging state and civil society configurations

Underlying national histories and narratives are important in enabling or constraining options for change, but they become all the more significant when they are expressed through institutions that have both democratic legitimacy and the powers to act. This section explores the ways in which different factors – history and culture, the economy and public expenditure, state institutions, policy-making and governance – are fusing to produce particular configurations of state and civil society in the respective countries of the UK and what this could mean for the processes of convergence and divergence.

History, culture and political direction

Earlier chapters have discussed the importance of the different histories and contexts of the four nations. These differences now assume increasing importance. Throughout the book, England as an entity has not really been discussed because of the political equation of England with the UK Westminster Government. There is an English education and training system, but there is not an English political system. Moreover, the English have not so far seemed inclined to develop their own political system and rejected moves to create a more explicit regional government tier in 2006 (ESRC, 2005; Trench, 2009). With the UK as a political entity being subjected to greater pressures, however, the nature of Englishness and the issue of regionalism may become more visible, but this debate is still in its infancy.

Scotland, on the other hand, has a strong, historically-based national identity, which has been further strengthened by parliamentary devolution and the rise of the Scottish National Party (SNP) as a political force. Keating (2005) argues that parliamentary devolution did not create an entirely new situation, but built on existing administrative devolution where 'policies could be adapted for local contexts' (Ozga, 2005: 124). The election of the SNP, however, as a minority government in 2007 heightened expectations of a more distinctive Scottish politics and, as Raffe (2009) records, it has adopted a clearly focused political strategy aimed at sustainable economic growth.

Wales is smaller and in some respects less distinct, but here too there is a growing sense of Welsh politics and culture, a more visible indigenous language with statutory support and a consciousness of national needs (Loughlin and Sykes, 2004). In Chapter 4, Gareth Rees argues that while Wales does not have the same powers as Scotland, this has not prevented it from developing a distinctive policy agenda, particularly in relation to education and training.

As we have seen in Chapter 1, Northern Ireland is a different case again and in some respects unique. It has two communities – Protestant and Catholic – which have looked in different national directions and have come into conflict over this. However, a peace process appears to be well underway, powers have been devolved to the Stormont Government and 'bread and butter' politics may be replacing sectarian politics, although it still might not be regarded as a 'normal society' (Wilson and Meehan, 2008). There is also growing support from both communities for more devolved powers (ESRC, 2005). Moreover, the relationship between Northern Ireland and the UK is changing, not only because of these underlying political movements but also, as we will see, due to the wider effects of the recessions and the UK Coalition's economic policies. Northern Ireland is also particularly dependent on the public sector for employment.

In the cases of Scotland and Wales, historical differences have been played out in relation to the direction of state and political development during the last 30 years. Not only has this included the resistance and mediation of Thatcherite new public management reforms, but also of New Labour's more adaptive neo-liberal versions. Viewed historically from the 1970s onwards, it is England that changed while Wales and Scotland held a steadier course, retaining the features of a Keynsian post-war settlement that fitted with their core values. Furthermore, from a wider European perspective England, despite its dominance within the UK, could be seen as the neo-liberal deviant and Scotland and Wales as more mainstream.

The economy and public expenditure

In several fundamental respects, the economy and the development of skills is a force for convergence and integration of the four countries. What is being debated, however, is how economies should be run, the role of the state and the public sector and the levels of funding for these to be effective. Central to this issue has been the so-called Barnett Formula, which guides the distribution of public monies between the four countries. Based on a range of factors including economic activity, unemployment, health, rurality and security issues, per capita expenditure has been significantly higher for Scotland, Wales and Northern Ireland than for England, although within England, expenditure is higher for poorer regions such as the North East compared with the more affluent London and the South East (BBC, 2010b). The Barnett Formula could thus be seen as a force for convergence because moves to greater financial autonomy would risk a reduction in the level of public expenditure in Scotland, Wales and Northern Ireland, unless these countries raised more in revenue from their own populations and economies. Unsurprisingly, it is a source of controversy in all four countries and there has been constant pressure in Westminster to reassess resource distribution. This issue will be brought into very sharp relief as a result of the proposed austerity measures by the UK Coalition Government because public expenditure reductions will hit Scotland, Wales and Northern Ireland particularly hard, not only because of the Barnett Formula, but also because the private sector is weaker in these countries and less able to fill the gap left by a shrinking state.

Under New Labour, growing public expenditure allowed divergence to take place in areas such as teachers' pay and tuition fees because of the financial ability to pay for these. Devolution developed in a relatively benign economic environment (Jeffrey *et al.*, 2010). Conversely, austerity could prove to be a force for convergence as everyone is compelled to cut back provision. However, faced with a pro-choice, pro-charging and pro-privatisation of services agenda from the UK Coalition Government, there could be demands for more devolved powers to deal with the situation according to the prevailing values of the respective nations. In Scotland, for example, there are now calls from the SNP for full fiscal autonomy, sometimes referred to as 'devolution max' (Jeffrey *et al.*, 2010), that would allow a Scottish Government to raise all their main taxes, including personal income tax, corporation tax, VAT and excise duties (SNP News, 2010). Plaid Cymru (2010) has called for a fairer funding deal for Wales. The looming economic crisis could eventually result in macro-economic powers being ceded to Scotland, Wales and Northern Ireland in order to head off a wider political revolt. As a result, they would accrete more state-like features.

State institutions, policy-making and governance

In earlier chapters we have argued that the most significant areas of divergence are to be found in relation to governance, organisation and policy-making. This is where parliamentary devolution has provided the space for different structures, practices and ideological preferences to consolidate. They are also sources of potential divergence in the future as they bring different perspectives and political logics to new external challenges.

It is becoming clear that distinctive state and civil society configurations are emerging in Scotland and Wales, when compared to England. At the centre of these are democratically elected parliaments or assemblies, which have been accumulating powers over different areas of economic, social and political life, although these powers are still limited and do not cover the critical dimensions of state activity such as defence and security, tax raising and the conduct of the media (Keating, 2005). HM Treasury, for example, still has overall responsibility for managing the UK economy. Political devolution to date could thus be seen to have resulted in the ceding of powers to key areas of civil society as part of the extended state, but not to important areas of the central and governmental state upon which power can be seen fundamentally to rest. The current state and civil society configurations in Scotland and Wales mean that these countries remain 'partially-stated nations'.

However, there are important differences between Scotland, Wales and Northern Ireland in terms of their acquisition of state powers. Trench (2009) reminds us that Wales only has executive devolution with an incremental and patchwork growth of legislative powers, whereas Scotland has both legislative and executive devolution. Moreover, he argues that Scotland has a more highly developed civil society in which the professions and educational institutions are stronger. In Wales, local government and the trade unions play a more prominent role. At the level of the governmental state, notably in the area of security, Northern Ireland has been more closely integrated into the UK. This is both the result and cause of conflict. More recently, however, distinctive institutions have been introduced by the 'Good Friday Agreement' in order to encourage a new settlement between the communities and relationships with Westminster and the Government in the Republic of Ireland.

While there are differences between the small nations in terms of the power of government, there are significant divergences between Scotland and Wales on the one hand, and England, on the other, in relation to the balance between national and local government. Local government has a more active and legitimate role in Scotland and Wales, where it has been a permanent part of the political landscape over several decades, whereas in England the role of local government has broadly diminished over the last 30 years despite its partial rehabilitation by New Labour since 2006. By the same token, quangos play less of a role in Wales and, to some extent, in Scotland.

In England, unelected non-departmental public bodies (NDPBs) have had an increasingly important place in steering policy and in creating a direct link between central government and provider institutions such as schools and colleges. In doing so, they have deployed a range of policy steers to influence provider and professional behaviour, bypassing the role of local government (Coffield *et al.*, 2008). This is part of a more global neo-liberal phenomenon of 'agencification' (Christensen and Laegreid, 2006) with the UK, or more precisely England, having played an outrider role.

In Scotland and Wales, therefore, there is a greater sense of 'government', rather than 'governance'. In the Welsh case, what was referred to as a 'bonfire of the quangos' in the period since parliamentary devolution in 1999 brought important powers within the remit of the Welsh Assembly Government (Loughlin and Sykes, 2004). However, the issue of quangos still attracts controversy in Scotland, with pledges from the Scottish Government to prune the number of NDPBs from 199 to 161 (Herald Scotland, 2010). Democratic reformers are, nevertheless, calling for far more radical measures (e.g. Reform Scotland, 2010). Regardless of the role of quangos, as we have seen in Chapters 3 and 4, there is a more direct relationship between democratically elected politicians, civil service officials, local government and other stakeholders in Scotland and Wales. Size plays its part. These smaller systems permit a more intimate approach to policy-making and enactment, with the oft-quoted myth of all relevant policy-makers being able to meet in one room. As part of a climate of greater openness, the Welsh Assembly Government has been much more accessible to a wide range of stakeholders than under the old Welsh Office, representing a 'sea change' in attitude (Loughlin and Sykes, 2004).

Different approaches to policy-making, however, do not simply result from size; they are influenced by political perspectives and prevailing narratives. The traditional view of Scottish policy-making is that it is underpinned by public provision, consensus, partnership, consultation, informality and incrementalism (Raffe, 2005, 2009). It is also a part of Scottish tradition to accord respect to the expert professional voice (Ozga, 2005). Critics, however, suggest that this can result in policy 'cosiness', with a reliance on professional and administrative elites (Paterson, 2003). Raffe (2009) argues that this contributes to 'autonomous' policy-making because of narratives that policy elites are able to generate. However, he also suggests that Scottish policy-making is reactive because it treats England as a reference point to highlight differences. Given the fact that a sovereign UK government in Westminster invariably has the initiative (Trench, 2009), what has occurred in Scotland and Wales could be seen as a mixture of reactive and autonomous policy-making.

While autonomous policy-making in Wales has a shorter history, Welsh national identity has been strengthened by the post-1999 institutions that promote core values of communitarianism and egalitarianism. These are linked to historical traditions of religious non-conformity, the strength of the trade union movement and the legacy of heavy industry (Loughlin and Sykes, 2004). Broader political and cultural narratives manifest themselves in, for example, the reform of public services. In a comparison of Welsh and English approaches to public service delivery, Brand (2007) noted that both English and Welsh policy-makers sought to produce more citizen-centred services, but conceptualised this in quite different ways. The English approach, reflected in *The local government White Paper* (DCLG, 2006), envisaged citizen engagement as part of a more market- and choice-based strategy, focused on cost reduction and efficiency. The Welsh Assembly Government's *Beyond Boundaries* (2006), on the other hand, placed much more emphasis on the citizen as central to the design of services with a focus on co-production.

While Scottish and Welsh approaches to policy and policy-making within the emerging state structures are becoming increasingly distinctive, they can also have a mythological quality. Raffe (2009) refers to 'narrative privilege' in which there is a prevailing sense of a Scottish way of doing things. This, he argued, assumes a consensus about purpose, tends towards complacency and does not always challenge power relationships and hierarchies. Similar mythologies also arise in Wales. Here policy-making could be viewed as 'aspirational'. Reflecting core values, there is a search for a more democratic and participative approach to policy and policy-making. However, the transfer of powers from quangos to the Welsh Assembly Government and the lack of strategic capacity within a small political system has meant that certain professional groups have been able to take advantage of a more open political process, resulting in a growing influence of established professional elites (Rees, 2004).

The overall effect of the historical, economic, political and ideological dimensions discussed above has been to consolidate political structures in the three small countries, which are more firmly focused on 'public value' than is the English structure. While the extent of democratisation of their state structures is debatable, the particular state/civil society mixes allow for an increasingly wider range of voices to be heard.

Conceptualising different state and civil society configurations

These different configurations of state, civil society, policy-making and democracy in the respective countries of the UK can be conceptualised by looking at the way in which they combine hierarchy, markets and networks (Rhodes, 1997). Pratchett (2009) observed that it is tempting to view local government and governance over the last 30 years as a historical progression from government hierarchies (pre-1980s), through to market-based relationships (1980s), to contemporary forms of network governance such as partnerships, which have been a feature of the governance landscape over the last decade or so, notably in England. The reality is that all three governance structures co-exist. The question is their relationship and which ones are more influential in shaping policy and practice.

Using a model designed to discuss different versions of 'localism' (Hodgson and Spours, 2010), it is possible broadly to situate the different respective state/civil society configurations in the four countries of the UK along the axes of centralisation/decentralisation and markets/public value.

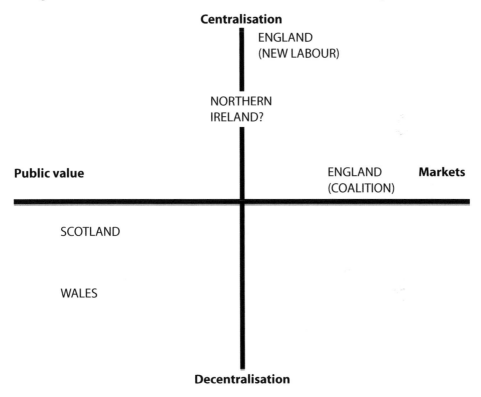

Figure 7.1: State formation: A framework of analysis

In the case of *England*, the relationship between hierarchy, markets and networks has been principally shaped by the role of central government (or more precisely ministers), policy steering mechanisms and marketised institutions. This classical new public management approach of the 1980s and early 1990s bypassed the 'hierarchy' of local government through marketisation and privatisation. New Labour's adaptive version of neo-liberalism (Newman, 2001) introduced a greater range of policy steers (Coffield *et al.*, 2008), more layers (local government came back more into the picture) and latterly, networking in the form of partnerships to promote the delivery of more effective public services. However, New Labour's late conversion to 'localism' did not reverse its earlier centralism or the marketisation of previous Conservative administrations.

England (or more precisely the UK state which governs England) could thus be broadly situated on the top-right quadrant of Figure 7.1 insofar as it has a state formation that has been largely structured over the last three decades by centralisation and markets. New Labour could be seen to have pulled a little towards the public value and decentralisation quadrant with its investment in public services and more latterly with its support for local government, but these social democratic tendencies were always subordinate to the more dominant neo-liberal strands of its policy (Hall, 2003). The new UK Coalition Government actively promotes markets and has, at the same time, gestured in the direction of decentralisation with a promise to cut back quangos (The Prime Minister's Office, 2010). It appears to favour networks as part of its 'Big Society' concept, but views them as 'anti-state' – a substitute for much of local government activity and contributor to local market-making (Respublica, 2010). Moreover, the exercise of ministerial power in the area of education in particular appears undiminished. The UK Coalition Government, therefore, could be situated more towards the bottom right-hand quadrant, but it remains to be seen whether it will genuinely wish to relinquish central power.

At the same time, research and policy debates within England have had a radical edge, although they have yet to fully break through at the political level. A more explicitly neo-liberal policy environment has generated a specific set of governance debates which, over the last ten years, have explored looser networking forms of governance as a response to top-down policy steering and the more active role of markets in policy formation. The concept of the 'New Localism', for example, has been promoted by the New Local Government Network (e.g. Filkin *et al.*, 2000) and by key academics, such as Pratchett (2004), Stoker (2004) and Skelcher *et al.* (2005). The New Localism envisages not only an active role for local government, but greater powers being devolved to communities and other parts of civil society. Mindful of the dangers of localism that might accentuate fragmentation and social differences embedded in localities, it is recognised that the devolution of powers has to take place within supportive local, regional and national frameworks that promote coordination and equity. More recently, localism has been developed in relation to education and lifelong learning through a number of related concepts – strongly collaborative local learning systems (Hodgson and Spours, 2006), local learning ecologies (Hodgson and Spours, 2009), and devolved social partnership applied to the world of learning and skills (Coffield *et al.*, 2008) – that analyse how a range of different institutions could collaborate to promote learner inclusion and progression in a local area.

In *Scotland* and *Wales*, the greater acceptance of the role of local government and different approaches to policy-making and citizen involvement in public service delivery, suggest a configuration of hierarchy, markets and networks more situated in the public realm and which gives greater credence to democratically elected structures. The partial states of Scotland and Wales could, therefore, be situated broadly on the left-hand side of the model in Figure 7.1 and towards the bottom quadrants, although not in identical positions. Their precise locations will depend on the degree of democratization of the emerging state/civil society configurations – the range of powers ceded from Westminster, the openness of their national governments, the degree of powers afforded to local government, the role of policy elites and how far communities and a variety of social partners participate and shape the delivery of services. Taking into consideration the 'traditional' and 'alternative' view of policy-making in Scotland and Wales, their systems could be seen to be a mix of traditional hierarchies and networks with a strong role for public value and a weaker position for markets. As we have seen in Chapter 3, traditional interpretations of the importance of local government in Scotland, as in the area of policy-making, are questioned.

Northern Ireland is more difficult to place on this model due to the fact that the devolved government is at a much earlier stage of development and because of complications in its internal politics. It is possible, however, that state, market and democratic configurations in Northern Ireland could place it somewhere within the top quadrants, because of the moves to centralise government organisations in order to facilitate power-sharing. Northern Ireland's dependency on public expenditure, on the other hand, might pull it away from the marketised end of the markets/public value continuum.

State formation, political narratives and policy directions

The state and political systems of the UK are reaching a watershed, and it is these wider developments that will shape public services, including the future of post-compulsory education and lifelong learning. Let us first consider the three smaller countries and three new shaping influences – the economy, extended state/civil society formations and the changing role of political parties – that will overlay existing historical and cultural backgrounds.

First, as those involved in Clinton's successful 1992 presidential campaign realised when looking at what influenced elections: 'it's the economy, stupid'. We may be moving from an era in which divergence was defined largely by different emphases on governance and organisation to one marked by competing approaches to the economy. The three devolved parliaments and assemblies have become established, enjoy increasing legitimacy and will attempt to gather greater powers of discretion, not least because of demands for the means to cope with the economic difficulties that lie ahead. In Scotland and Wales, in particular, there may be different views to those prevailing in Westminster on the balance of tax-raising and spending cuts and where funding priorities lie. The battle lines will thus be drawn around the relationship between state and markets, in the context of a relatively weak private sector and a UK Coalition Government project to shrink the public state. Nevertheless, options for public services will also be heavily determined by diminishing economic resources. Whether this results in everyone becoming a neo-liberal under duress, or whether it forces out underlying political values, remains to be seen. On balance, it may well be the latter as the different political communities across the UK not only oppose Westminster, but also look for more democratic and cost-effective ways of organising public services. Emerging experiments involving the mutualist organisation of local services are explored briefly in the final section of this chapter.

Second, the accumulating changes to governance and the changing political complexions will also shape options. Despite the continued role of policy elites, Scotland, Wales and Northern Ireland are, in their different ways, committed to democratic projects, either as a result of already existing governance developments or underlying political narratives concerned with egalitarianism and the public realm. In the case of Northern Ireland, its democratic project is tied to power-sharing between the communities and to conflict resolution. Despite the constraining effect of reducing public expenditure, substantial community commitment to the idea of the public sector and public value, combined with greater opportunities to participate in the policy process, may fuel further divergence in all three countries. The more states become extended due to the expanded role of civil society, the greater the opportunities for different social partners to meet to forge a more distinctive politics.

The third factor is party political. During the past 13 years, New Labour invested a great deal of political capital in orchestrating a carefully managed process of divergence. Differences were accepted, although they were often in less visible areas of state life. While recent years saw the waning of the New Labour star in Scotland and Wales, coalition and minority governments have reinforced this devolution process. The election of a UK Conservative–Liberal Democrat Coalition, however, totally changes the political dynamic. The upcoming assembly and parliamentary elections in Wales and Scotland in 2011 could see a resurgent Labour Party and the Nationalists fighting for the leadership role in opposing the Westminster agenda. While David Cameron may wish for a relationship between the UK Government and the three assemblies and parliaments based on an 'agenda of respect' (BBC, 2010c), he may find this difficult to achieve. The Scottish and Welsh Governments will not take kindly to the destruction of cherished services and projects by a UK Government which, they feel, has little legitimacy in their countries. Despite growing differences, the governments of Scotland, Wales and Northern Ireland will have to engage with the UK Government. It is difficult though to see where lasting agreement will come from.

Beyond convergence and divergence: A post-independence politics?

It is possible to view the last ten years as a form of 'managed divergence' in which New Labour, responding to the demands of parliamentary devolution, reached a set of understandings that provided for differences in key policy areas to emerge between the four countries of the UK. The Labour Government and the Labour Party had a clear political incentive to maintain predictable and stable relationships within this growing diversity.

We now appear, however, to be entering an era of uncertainty because of a new constellation of factors – the election of a UK Coalition Government with little support in Scotland and Wales; an austerity budget which will disproportionately affect those areas of the UK that depend most on the public sector; and accumulated differences of policy perspective between Scotland and Wales, on the one hand, and the UK Government on the other. While reduced public spending could force more common economic disciplines across the four nations, the underlying dynamics of state and civil society and ideology and politics are pressures for greater divergence in a period in which the management of the economy threatens to totally dominate the agenda.

Should divergence be welcomed? From a democratic perspective, it is important that different peoples and nations are able to articulate a settled will. Policy divergence, understood as autonomous policy-making, may be a reflection of this. Similarly, divergence may be the result of reactive policy-making, operating as a rejection or mediation of initiatives from a dominant Westminster. Differences can be regarded as proof that devolution is working (Jeffrey et al., 2010).

While it will be impossible for political control to be imposed from the centre and, as we will see in Chapter 8, much of Coalition policy will have little traction in Scotland and Wales, a real threat will come from 'arm's length' control via the vehicle of public expenditure. In effect, devolution could become the devolution of financial pain as the UK Coalition Government attempts to impose, by remote mechanisms, the logic of the market. Relationships between Westminster and the three countries may thus get much worse before they have the chance to get better.

Nevertheless, relationships matter and we should be concerned to explore more fully what has been termed a 'post-devolution politics' (Hassan, 2010). This suggests going beyond the local inflection or mediation of policy from Westminster (Ozga, 2005), to a new level of sharing, understanding and learning between the nations. While relationships are going to be extremely tense in the medium term, some are thinking beyond the looming impasse towards a new settlement. Hassan (2010), for example, argues from a Scottish perspective 'that we could embrace a politics of post-nationalist independence and inter-independence, which would entail Scotland developing new arrangements with the other nations of the UK, sharing sovereignty, and recognising the importance of the English dimension'. More concretely, he suggests that demands for greater devolved powers open up the possibility of a future settlement in which a devolved administration will want to negotiate with the central government an agreed share for paying for common services such as defence and to develop an economic model of federalism along Spanish/Basque lines. Wales may aspire to follow this direction but, as a smaller and poorer nation, the timelines may be longer and, at least in the medium term, the powers more limited. Others (e.g. Trench, 2009) are more sceptical about a Spanish scenario because of the asymmetry between a large and dominant England and the smaller three countries.

A UK-wide approach is certainly needed in economically related areas. In terms of post-compulsory education and lifelong learning, there is a strong case for a new set of relationships based on UK-wide approaches to key policy areas, for example to employment policy and skills, access to higher education and the transportability of qualifications across national boundaries. Moreover, all four countries are part of a wider EU agenda, although this appears less influential than in many continental European systems.

There is also a strong case for more effective policy learning across the different systems which, despite divergence, share a UK economy and still tend to conceptualise issues in a somewhat UK way. However, as pointed out earlier, there is currently little inclination for the other nations to include England in this process – or indeed vice versa – because of glaring political differences. If policy learning and greater sharing is to take place, there would need to be much more common political ground between the nations – or perhaps greater maturity in recognising the potential scope for policy learning despite political differences – than there is presently. Devolution creates a great deal of creativity and this needs to be harnessed more systematically (Jeffrey et al., 2010).

A new stage of post-devolution politics may thus rest on two conditions. First, the three smaller countries accept that England has to be part of a new settlement and that the process of divergence and autonomy is not enough. As Pratchett (2004) argues, there is a qualitative difference between 'freedom from' and 'freedom to'. One is about distance from a higher and more powerful force, the other is about the sharing of powers to act collectively to transform localities or, in this case, the nations that currently constitute the UK.

The second condition involves a shift in the debate, particularly in England. Here, a harsher and more conservative climate of public opinion about welfare and the role of the public sector is forcing sections of the Left to think more about concepts of 'reciprocity' that link services, personal contribution and popular participation to the concept of fairness (e.g. White, 2010). It has been argued that it will be difficult for the Labour Party to be re-elected in England by simply promising to re-expand the state. Imaginative democratic solutions are needed (e.g. Painter, 2010; Lawson, 2010) to counter the Coalition's version of localism. In this respect, interesting and competing ideas about the role of local government, mutualisation and popular participation have been emerging, for example the John Lewis or EasyCouncil models of local services (Stratton, 2010). During a period of dramatic public expenditure cuts and the expected arrival of what can be termed the 'austerity state', it is possible that radical ideas and developments at the local level across all the countries of the UK could open the door to a new era of policy learning.

References

Bain, D. (2010) 'The Left in Scotland'. In M. Power (ed.), *Left Out: Alternative policies for the Left opposition today*. London: LW ebooks. <http://www. lwbooks.co.uk/ebooks/leftout.html> (accessed 10 September 2010).

Ball, S. J. (1990) *Politics and Policymaking in Education: Explorations in Policy Sociology*. London: Routledge.

Brand, A. (2007) *Devolution and Divergence: Comparing English and Welsh approaches to citizen-centred public service delivery*. London: New Local Government Network.

British Broadcasting Corporation (BBC) (2010a) 'Tories were "wrong" on devolution'. 27 June. <http://news.bbc.co.uk/1/hi/uk_politics/8122065.stm> (accessed 10 September 2010).

-- (2010b) 'Spending cuts to hit North harder'. <http://www.bbc.co.uk/news/ uk-england-11141264> (accessed 11 September 2010).

-- (2010c) 'Cameron calls for Scot's "Respect"'. BBC News 14 May. <http://news. bbc.co.uk/1/hi/scotland/8680816.stm> (accessed 11 September 2010).

Christensen, T. and Laegreid, P. (eds) (2006) *Autonomy and Regulation: Coping with agencies in the modern state*. Cheltenham: Edward Elgar.

Coffield, F., Edward, S., Finlay, I., Hodgson, A., Spours, K. and Steer, R. (2008) *Improving Learning, Skills and Inclusion: The impact of policy on post-compulsory education*. London: Routledge.

Crabb, S. (2007) 'The devolution experiment is leading to socialism and separatism'. Conservativehome/Platform. <http://conservativehome.blogs.com/platform/2007/10/stephen-crabb-m.html> (accessed 10 September 2010).

Department for Communities and Local Government (DCLG) (2006) *Strong and Prosperous Communities: The local government White Paper*. Cm 6939. London: DCLG.

Economic and Social Research Council (ESRC) (2005) *Devolution Programme Report*. <http://www.devolution.ac.uk/final_report.htm> (accessed 10 September 2010).

Fairclough, N. (2000) *New Labour, New Language?*. London: Routledge.

Filkin, G., Stoker, G., Wilkinson, G. and Williams, J. (2000) *Towards a New Localism: Discussion paper*. London: New Local Government Network.

Hall, S. (2003) 'New Labour's double shuffle'. London: LW ebook, Soundings. <http://www.lwbooks.co.uk/journals/articles/nov03.html> (accessed 12 August 2010).

Hassan, G. (2010) 'The next Scottish constitutional revolution: Why Calman isn't the answer'. *Open Democracy*, <http://www.opedemocracy.net/ourkingdon/gerry_hassa/scotlands_independence_referendum> (accessed 19 October 2010).

Herald Scotland (2009) 'Cameron: Tories wrong to oppose Scots devolution'. <http://www.heraldscotland.com/cameron-tories-wrong-to-oppose-scots-devolution-1.913444> (accessed 10 September 2010).

-- (2010) 'Swinney wins backing to axe Scotland's quangos'. 25 March. <http://www.heraldscotland.com/news/politics/swinney-wins-backing-to-axe-scotland-s-quangos-1.1016141> (accessed 11 September 2010).

Hodgson, A. and Spours, K. (2006) 'An analytical framework for policy engagement: The contested case of 14–19 reform in England'. *Journal of Education Policy*, 21(6), 679–96.

-- (2009) *Collaborative Local Learning Ecologies: Reflections on the Governance of Lifelong Learning in England*. IFLL Sector Paper 6. NIACE <http://shop.niace.org.uk/ifll-sector-paper-6.html> (accessed 2 December 2009).

-- (2010) *Three Versions of 'Localism': Implications for upper secondary education and lifelong learning in the UK*. Paper presented to the European Conference on Educational Research Conference, Helsinki, 27 August.

Holliday, I. (1992) 'Scottish limits to Thatcherism'. *The Political Quarterly*, 63(4), 448–59.

Jeffery, C., Lodge, G. and Schmuecker, K. (2010) 'The devolution paradox'. In G. Lodge and K. Schmuecker (eds), *Devolution in Practice 2010: Public policy differences in the UK*. London: IPPR.

Jessop, B. (1999) 'The dynamics of partnership and governance failure'. In G. Stoker (ed.), *The New Politics of Local Governance in Britain*. Macmillan: Basingstoke.

Keating, M. (2005) 'Policy convergence and divergence in Scotland under devolution'. *Regional Studies*, 39(4), 453–63.

Lawson, N. (2010) 'We need to rethink the role of the state'. In J. Rutherford and A. Lockey (eds) *Labour's Future*. London: LW ebook, Soundings. <http://www.lwbooks.co.uk/ebooks/laboursfuture.html> (accessed 11 September 2010).

Loughlin, J. and Sykes, S. (2004) *Devolution and Policy-making in Wales: Restructuring the system and reinforcing identity*. ESRC Devolution and Constitutional Change Programme. <http://www.devolution.ac.uk/Policy_Papers.htm> (accessed 11 September 2010).

Morgan, R. (2002) 'Making social policy in Wales'. Speech to the National Centre for Public Policy. University of Wales, Swansea, 11 December.

Newman, J. (2001) *Modernising Governance: New Labour, policy and society*. London: Sage/OUP.

Newman, J. and Clarke, J. (2009) *Publics, Politics and Power: Remaking the public in public services*. Sage: London.

Ozga, J. (2000) *Policy Research in Education Settings: Contested terrain*. Buckingham: Open University Press.

-- (2005) 'Travelled and embedded policy: The case of post-devolution Scotland within the UK'. In D. Coulby and E. Zambeta (eds), *Globalisation and Nationalism in Education*. World Yearbook of Education, 2005. Oxford: RoutledgeFalmer.

Painter, A. (2010) 'How should we respond to the austerity state?'. In J. Rutherford and A. Lockey (eds), *Labour's Future*. London: LW ebook, Soundings. <http://www.lwbooks.co.uk/ebooks/laboursfuture.html> (accessed 11 September 2010).

Paterson, L. (2003) 'The three educational ideologies of the British Labour Party, 1997–2001'. *Oxford Review of Education*, 29(2), 165–86.

Plaid Cymru (2010) 'Wales deserves a fair deal'. <http://www.plaidcymru.org/content.php?nID=14;ID=1411;lID=1> (accessed 11 September 2010).

Pratchett, L. (2004) 'Local autonomy, local democracy and the "new localism"'. *Political Studies*, 52(2), 358–75.

-- (2009) 'Local governance, local autonomy and local democracy: Towards a comparative framework.' Presentation for 'New Directions in Learning and Skills in England, Scotland and Wales' seminar, Institute of Education, University of London, 18 February. <http://www.tlrp.org/themes/documents/hodgsonsem2/LocalgovernanceautonomydemocracyPratchett.pdf> (accessed 11 September 2010).

Raffe, D. (2005) 'Devolution and divergence in education policy'. In J. Adams and K. Schmueker (eds), *Devolution in Practice 2006: Public policy differences within the UK*. Newcastle: IPPR, 52–69.

-- (2009) 'Devolution and governance: A Scottish perspective'. Presentation for 'New Directions in Learning and Skills in England, Scotland and Wales' seminar, Institute of Education, University of London, 18 February. <http://www.tlrp.org/themes/documents/hodgsonsem2/DevolutionandGovernanceaScottishperspectiveDavid%20Raffe.pdf> (accessed 10 September 2010).

Raffe, D. and Spours, K. (eds) (2007) *Policy-making and Policy Learning in 14–19 Education*. London: Institute of Education, University of London.

Raffe, D., Brannen, K., Croxford, L. and Martin, C. (1999) 'Comparing England, Scotland, Wales and Northern Ireland: The case for "home internationals"'. *Comparative Education*, 35(1), 9–25.

Rees, G. (2004) 'Democratic devolution and education policy in Wales: The emergence of a national system?'. *Contemporary Wales*, 17, 28–43.

Reform Scotland (2010) 'Think-tank urges abolition of quangos and contracted out services'. 2 February, <http://www.reformscotland.com/index.php/publication/view_details/682/> (accessed 11 September 2010).

Respublica (2010) 'Beyond localism: Rethinking British governance'. <http://www.respublica.org.uk/articles/beyond-localism-rethinking-british-governance> (accessed 12 September 2010).

Rhodes, R.A.W. (1997) *Understanding Governance: Policy networks, governance, reflexivity and accountability*. Buckingham: Open University Press.

Skelcher, C., Mathur, N. and Smith, M. (2005) 'The public governance of collaborative spaces: Discourse, design and democracy'. *Public Administration*, 83, 573–96.

SNP News (2010) 'SNP highlight Tory threat to public spending'. <http://www.snp.org/node/15933> (accessed 11 September 2010).

Stoker, G. (2004) *New Localism, Participation and Networked Community Governance*. University of Manchester. <http://www.ipeg.org.uk/papers/ngcnewloc.pdf> (accessed 12 August 2010).

Stratton, A. (2010) 'Labour to rebrand Lambeth as "John Lewis" council'. *The Guardian*, 17 February. <http://www.guardian.co.uk/politics/2010/feb/17/labour-rebrand-lambeth-john-lewis-council> (accessed 10 September 2010).

The Prime Minister's Office (2010) 'Queen's Speech: Decentralisation and Localism Bill'. <http://www.number10.gov.uk/queens-speech/2010/05/queens-speech-decentralisation-and-localism-bill-50673> (accessed 12 August 2010).

Trench, A. (2009) 'Devolution in Great Britain and the governance of learning and skills'. Presentation for 'New Directions in Learning and Skills in England, Scotland and Wales' seminar, Institute of Education, University of London, 18 February. <http://www.tlrp.org/themes/documents/hodgsonsem2/DevolutioninGBandtheGovernanceofLearningandSkillsAlanTrench.pdf> (accessed 19 October 2010).

Welsh Assembly Government (2006) *Beyond Boundaries: Citizen-centred local services for Wales*. Cardiff: Welsh Assembly Government.

White, S. (2010) 'The left and reciprocity'. In J. Rutherford and A. Lockey (eds), *Labour's Future*. London: LW ebook, Soundings. <http://www.lwbooks.co.uk/ebooks/laboursfuture.html> (accessed 11 September 2010).

Whitty, G. and Power, S. (2000) 'Marketization and privatization in mass education systems'. *International Journal of Educational Development*, 20(2), 93–107.

Wilson, R. and Meehan, E. (2008) 'Can Northern Ireland become normal? Attitudes to the role of government in Northern Ireland'. *ARK Research Update*, 57. <http://www.ark.ac.uk/publications/updates/update57.pdf> (accessed 10 September 2010).

Chapter 8

Post-compulsory education and lifelong learning across the UK: Moving from managed divergence to a new period of uncertainty

Ann Hodgson, Ken Spours, Martyn Waring, Jim Gallacher, Ewart Keep and Gareth Rees

Introduction

The writing and publication of this book has taken place at an important political juncture with the election of the new UK Conservative–Liberal Democrat Coalition Government. The book as a whole, and this chapter in particular, provides the opportunity to look back over the past two decades, which include successive Labour governments in Westminster and parliamentary devolution in Scotland, Wales and latterly in Northern Ireland. This was a period of considerable change in which post-compulsory education, skills and lifelong learning remained a high-profile policy area across all the countries of the UK because of its association with competitiveness in an increasingly globalised world economy and its role in supporting social inclusion (for example, Leitch, 2006; DEL, 2010), civic participation (for example, Webb Review, 2007) and the development of a fairer society (Scottish Government, 2007).

Reflecting on the period since 1999 and parliamentary devolution in Scotland and Wales, we discuss underlying trends influencing convergence and divergence of post-compulsory education and lifelong learning between the four countries of the UK. We then briefly examine the emerging policy framework from the new UK Coalition Government elected in May 2010 and its potential implications.

In the final part of the chapter, we outline scenarios that will help us explore two key questions:

1. From an assessment of the early messages emerging from the new UK Coalition Government, what is the likely direction of policy for post-compulsory education and lifelong learning?
2. Will the process of divergence identified in earlier chapters of the book increase as a result of UK-wide economic pressures?

We conclude by suggesting that what started out in the book as a discussion about convergence or divergence of policy in post-compulsory education and lifelong learning may become part of a much wider debate about the future of the UK state as a political entity.

The processes of convergence and divergence

Throughout the book we have highlighted similarities and differences between the post-compulsory education and lifelong learning systems of the UK. Overall, it could be argued that a process of divergence is taking place in a number of key areas between England on the one hand and Scotland and Wales on the other. It is more difficult to fully include Northern Ireland in this analysis because devolution has only been recently restored and there has been a very specific history of division between religious and political communities that powerfully affected the education system. Even here, however, according to Gallagher (2010), contrasting policy processes have begun to emerge between England and Northern Ireland, with the latter experiencing a more democratic style of policy development in relation to curriculum reform. Furthermore, proposed budget deficit strategies by the UK Coalition Government are likely to fuel tensions between the devolved government in Stormont and Westminster, with the major parties on either side of the sectarian divide (Democratic Unionist Party and Sinn Fein) in Northern Ireland, who now form the Northern Ireland Executive, having to work together to respond to deep cuts in public services (BBC, 2010).

As previous chapters have pointed out, this move towards greater divergence is underpinned by wider historical, cultural, economic and political factors in which the four countries of the UK have had different experiences of new public management, the role of local government and the balances of the public and private sectors. While England fully embraced the neo-liberal reforms associated with Conservative governments during the 1980s and early 1990s and, as we have seen, largely continued by New Labour, this was not the case for Scotland and Wales. They continued along their established broadly pre-Thatcherite trajectories. Interwoven with issues of national identity, these wider historical, cultural and political factors have affected underlying policy assumptions and become a framework for policy-makers in the respective countries, influencing how post-compulsory education and lifelong learning is conceptualised and even what terminology should be used.

The greatest areas of difference appear to be in relation to national and local governance arrangements and the ways that policy-making takes place, with greater affordances for the professional voice in Scotland, Wales and now possibly in Northern Ireland. Here size matters. The relatively small populations of Scotland (around 5 million), Wales (around 3 million) and Northern Ireland (less than 2 million) in comparison with England (around 51 million) create the potential for more collaborative working in the three smaller countries between ministers and their policy officials on the one hand and stakeholders with a direct interest in policy development on the other. As earlier chapters in the book have pointed out, it is possible for all providers to get into one room with the relevant policy-makers in these countries. There are also marked differences in the areas of qualifications and institutional collaboration, in which Wales and Scotland have moved in a more unified and less competitive direction than England or Northern Ireland. Moreover, the basis of the economy, the reliance on public expenditure and the role of the public sector in employment opportunities are different in Scotland, Wales and Northern Ireland when compared with England (particularly with London and the South East). This latter factor is likely to assume much greater importance in an era of recession and UK Government-imposed austerity.

On the other hand, we should not go too far with this line of argument. When viewed through an international lens, there are still considerable commonalities between the four countries of the UK, which might continue to limit divergence. These include the UK-wide labour market, the relatively weak role played by employers in the education and training system, and largely shared qualifications across England, Wales and Northern Ireland. Moreover, looking back over the period since 1997, it could be argued that there have been common themes of policy intervention in the four countries of the UK. Three stand out – an emphasis on raising skills levels, widening and increasing participation in learning and the use of qualifications as a key driver for change.

Nevertheless, the balance between divergence and convergence across the four countries is tipping towards the former. The underlying differences (in particular between England and Scotland and Wales) have been magnified through parliamentary devolution because education and training has been one of the areas in which national governments have been able to exercise policy preferences. These differences are likely to increase because of the accumulation of recent policies and changes to organisational structures, which affect the ways in which future policy options are interpreted – see, for example, Graystone (2010) on the direction of FE in Wales. An internal logic begins to take hold and a national narrative and accepted direction of travel become increasingly powerful in policy-making. This, in turn, can prompt demands for more devolved powers, for example to allow greater financial autonomy and capacity to determine investment priorities, which over time would provide scope for further divergence in policy development. Added to this are new factors related to the election of a Conservative–Liberal Democrat Coalition Government in Westminster, with its determination to substantially reduce public expenditure in order to tackle the budget deficit. These drastic measures will reveal the lack of macro-economic powers open to the devolved administrations (Bell, 2010), creating new points of tension between them and Westminster. The relationship between the four countries, their economies and (as one element of this) their education and training systems, thus appears more uncertain in this new political context.

The new UK Coalition Government policy approach: Early indications

While in 2010 economics and budget deficit reduction dominated the political landscape, the UK Conservative–Liberal Democrat Coalition made a very active start in the area of education and training in England. Its policies on creating a new generation of academies and a suite of Free Schools have grabbed the headlines, but behind these a number of early announcements on post-compulsory education, skills and lifelong learning point to important changes of emphasis as well as substance from the previous Labour Government.

Even at this early stage, it is possible to identify an emerging policy narrative and direction. In its initial statements, the Coalition appears to be significantly extending the previous Labour Government's emphasis on an education and training market, while attacking and reversing its managerialist approach (Cabinet Office, 2010). Moreover, it links the language of institutional autonomy and markets to fairness and tackling inequality, promoting lifelong learning, community and society in what is referred to as the 'post-bureaucratic age' (Chambers, 2010), all of which potentially resonate positively with education professionals. The recent Labour Government's record on performativity, accountability and micro-management, and its relative neglect of adult learning and inclusivity in England, have all provided opportunities for the Coalition to appeal to a range of audiences across the political spectrum.

Taking information from recent speeches, announcements and letters by ministers in the newly named ministries in England (the Department for Education and the Department for Business, Innovation and Skills) it is possible to identify four related strands of policy – curriculum and qualifications, organisation and governance, learners and providers, and Apprenticeships and the work-based route – that comprise the main aspects of the Coalition's new agenda in post-compulsory education and lifelong learning.

Curriculum and qualifications

Prior to the election of the Coalition Government, think tanks close to the Conservative Party (for example, Reform, Civitas and Policy Exchange) began publishing a number of influential policy documents on curriculum and qualifications (for example, Bassett *et al.*, 2009; Richmond and Freedman, 2009; De Waal, 2009). Subsequent to this, the Conservative Party established an 'independent' commission under Sir Richard Sykes to look at the future of GCSEs and A Levels for England (Conservative Party, 2010). Together, these reports supported a greater focus on subject disciplines and knowledge rather than skills; a move towards more linear GCSEs and A Levels; and the involvement of universities rather than quangos in the regulation and development of qualifications in England. More recently this support for traditional subjects and a concern for the decreasing number of 14–19 year olds studying science, history and modern and ancient languages has led the Secretary of State for Education, Michael Gove, to announce his desire to introduce a new 'English Baccalaureate' award for 16 year olds that recognises achievement in English, mathematics, one humanities subject, one science and one foreign language, either modern or ancient. Moreover, he hinted that in an overhaul of examination league tables, the English Baccalaureate would become one of the major ways of measuring school performance (Gove, 2010a).

One of the first announcements by Nick Gibb, Minister of State for Schools, halted the development of the 'Stage 4' Diploma lines in Humanities, Languages and Science and lifted restrictions on state schools in England offering the iGCSE, a qualification that has proved popular in independent schools (DfE, 2010a). This was followed by a speech to the Sixth Form Colleges' Forum in which he announced the decision to revoke the statutory requirement on local authorities in England to make the full suite of 14 Diplomas available to all learners in their locality (DfE, 2010b). Subsequently, Michael Gove has appointed Professor Alison Wolf, a recognised expert on vocational learning and a contributor to the Sykes Review, to lead a review of all vocational qualifications for 14–19 year olds (Gove, 2010b).

These changes, while presented by the Minister as part of schools and colleges in England being given 'greater freedom to offer the qualifications employers and universities demand', might also be seen as reflecting a desire to uphold a traditional approach to the study of academic disciplines. These freedoms, reinforced by the availability of new linear GCSE and A Level syllabuses, alongside the current modular variants, and the involvement of selector universities in qualifications development are likely to result in a division *within* general education in the English system. They will provide a basis that allows selector universities and courses to make offers contingent on students achieving high grades in linear syllabuses, providing that they are confident that sufficiently large numbers of high-performing students will take them. At the same time, the UK Coalition Government will strongly support Apprenticeships and established vocational qualifications such as BTEC and City and Guilds awards, with clearer routes from FE and Apprenticeship into higher education. The cumulative effects of these reforms could result in a redrawing of the binary divide in higher education in England, with a sharper division between academic and vocational pathways.

Organisation and governance

Potential divisions in the area of curriculum and qualifications in England may also be matched and supported by stronger delineation between different types of education provider. Michael Gove's first announcement (DfE, 2010c) as Secretary of State for Education focused on the creation of hundreds of new academies in England drawn primarily from the highest-attaining schools, both primary and secondary. The UK Coalition Government has also voiced its support for Lord Baker's idea to establish a number of university technical colleges (UTCs)/technical academies: 14–19 institutions focusing on vocational courses and Apprenticeships in particular sectors and supported by a local university (Cabinet Office, 2010). The first is to be established in Birmingham and supported by Aston University. It has since been suggested that UTCs may be a positive way forward for failing schools (Garner, 2010).

While the previous Labour Administration also established a number of academies in England, their purpose of replacing failing schools, largely in urban areas, with highly resourced institutions directly funded by Whitehall was very different. The UK Coalition Government policies in this area potentially recreate tripartism within the school system in England – academies become the new grammar schools, UTCs the new technical schools and the remaining maintained local authority schools, the secondary moderns. Together with the later announcement on the creation of 'Free Schools',[1] this approach to reform will further diversify the institutional landscape and could draw resources away from lower-performing schools that remain under local authority control.

More importantly for post-compulsory education and lifelong learning in England, these announcements are likely to lead to an increase in the number of small sixth forms in academies and to greater competition between colleges, schools and sixth form colleges for high-attaining students and scarce resources. Not only does the introduction of new and competing institutions make the English system more complex and divided at the age of 16, it also risks it becoming less efficient and less equitable. Higher achievers are more likely to be able to study at the institution of their choice, whereas many lower achievers will be channelled towards general further education colleges, where in England funding has been, and will probably continue to be, less generous.

In relation to governance arrangements, the UK Coalition Government has started with its own 'bonfire of the quangos', which it justifies via financial and anti-bureaucracy arguments (Cable, 2010). In the area of education and training in England, to date it has abolished a number of quangos, including the Teachers' Development Agency (TDA), the Qualifications and Curriculum Development Agency (QCDA), and the General Teaching Council (GTC). There was also talk before the election of a new funding agency, similar to the old FEFC, which would simplify the 'quangocracy' for post-compulsory education and lifelong learning in England (Conservative Party, 2008). In the event, the Young People's Learning Agency (YPLA) has been made responsible for funding 14–19 education and training in FE colleges, sixth form colleges and other training providers directly, while local authorities retain the strategic overview of provision and needs in this area, as well as responsibility for funding schools and school sixth forms (Gove, 2010c). This leaves the Skills Funding Agency (SFA), which is housed within the Department for Business, Innovation and Skills, responsible for funding 19+ education and training outside higher education. These arrangements effectively reduce the role of local authorities in 14–19 education and training, while apparently leaving the 'quangocracy' inherited from the Labour Government largely intact, at least for the time being. There is also an emerging sense that the UK Coalition Government is less wedded to the idea of a distinct 14–19 phase than the previous government.

On the other hand, much has already been said by the Coalition about transferring power from national government to localities and the people. However, its plans, as so far revealed, suggest an interesting tension between 'freedom' and control, and between what the DfE conceives of as freedom, and how the concept might be interpreted by ministers. Michael Gove's 'freedom' for schools (from local authority control) comes at the price of even greater powers for the Secretary of State for Education. As Peter Newsam noted in a letter to the *Guardian*:

> *It will give this, and any future education secretary in England, unprecedented powers, exercisable without reference to any elected body; opening a school whenever he wants; deciding where any individual school should be built; funding any school he likes on any terms he chooses, or, after due notice, ceasing to fund any school contracted to him whenever he likes…The untrammelled concentration of power in the hands of a single government minister was what the Butler Education Act of 1944, now effectively dismantled in a couple of days, was careful to avoid.*
>
> (Newsam, 2010: 33)

Learners and providers

The key message from the UK Coalition Government in the first few months of taking office has been that institutional autonomy and freedom from bureaucracy will allow schools and colleges in England to respond better to the needs of their local communities. In terms of post-compulsory education and lifelong learning, John Hayes (Minister for Further Education and Lifelong Learning) and Vince Cable (Secretary of State for the Department for Business, Innovation and Skills) made a number of speeches in support of the FE sector and adult and community learning (for example, Cable, 2010; Hayes, 2010a). FE is seen as the main provider of vocational education and skills development, of support for employers and Apprenticeships and community learning, and as playing an increasingly important role in higher education (Willetts, 2010).

The new Government has also sent a clear message to the FE sector in England that it wants to facilitate a stronger professional voice in policy-making via a range of bodies such as the Association of Learner Providers, the Association of Colleges and FE Principals' Network (Hayes, 2010b), although this does not appear to extend to the teacher and lecturer unions. The advice of sector managers will be sought, particularly around ways of reducing costs and bureaucracy.

With regard to learners, the UK Coalition Government intends to introduce Lifelong Learning Accounts in England and to have a stronger focus on adult information, advice and guidance, to ensure that potential learners' needs are better served in what is regarded as a growing post-16 educational marketplace. There will also be a greater emphasis on higher education students studying near to home, on creating partnerships between FE colleges and universities, for example via arrangements such as the London University External Programme, and on supporting new progression routes between further education, Apprenticeship and higher education (Willetts, 2010).

Apprenticeships and the work-based route

While all UK governments over the last two decades have stressed the importance of Apprenticeships, as we have seen earlier, the work-based route has played a relatively minor role in expanding participation in education and training for 16–19 year olds. This Government, like others before it, wants to see the work-based route making up a larger proportion of the education and training system. So it too has highlighted the key role of Apprenticeships (Conservative Party, 2008; Cabinet Office, 2010). It justifies this in terms of the benefits of skills acquisition and returns to learning that can be accrued from close learner engagement with the world of work. To this end, one of the first actions of the new administration has been to redirect £150 million from Train to Gain (a scheme in England for incentivising employers to engage in training) to Apprenticeships in order to provide 50,000 extra places for young people. This is a somewhat different approach from that taken by the previous government, in which a range of work-related and college-led courses were rebadged as Apprenticeships in order to raise the status of vocational programmes and to reach targets for growth in this area. An increasing role for the work-based route in England is also consistent with the UK Coalition Government's policy on general qualifications. It could be seen as providing an alternative form of education and training for those unwilling or unable to participate in a more 'rigorous' and narrowly cast academic route.

Whatever policies the UK Coalition Government wishes to introduce, however, will be largely shaped by the wider economy and its approach to reducing the public debt. While funding for 16–19 year olds will be protected in 2010/11, it is likely that post-compulsory education and lifelong learning will experience serious cuts in funding from 2011/12 onwards and will be directly affected by the condition of the labour market. We will argue towards the end of this chapter that the prevailing economic climate, and the UK Coalition Government's response to it, will have a major shaping effect on potential scenarios for the future.

The UK Coalition Government's impact on the devolved administrations

It is important to reiterate the point that these changes in UK Government policy directly affect only England of the countries of the UK. It remains to be seen how far the policies of the devolved administrations will be influenced by the new direction taken by the Coalition Government at Westminster. Here, the crucial issue will be the extent to which they will be able to 'insulate' their jurisdictions from the policies being implemented in England, especially now that the ideological gap between them is likely to be even greater than it has been hitherto. Indeed, it seems likely that education and training policies will provide one arena in which any new dynamic between Westminster and the governments in Edinburgh, Cardiff and Belfast will be worked out – or, perhaps, fought over.

More specifically, in the case of Wales, future relationships between the two governments are likely to be even more complex than they have been to date. Some of the changes being introduced in England will have an immediate impact in Wales. For example, many students in Wales take GCSEs and A Levels administered by examining authorities based in England; and it is unclear how far the Welsh Assembly Government and the Welsh Joint Examinations Council will pursue curriculum strategies significantly different from those adopted in England, although this is certainly possible. To the extent that the latter occurs, however, Welsh developments are likely to produce more porous boundaries between academic and vocational learning, under the auspices of the 14–19 Learning Pathways and providing further impetus to the Welsh Baccalaureate Qualification.

Certainly, it seems very unlikely that organisational changes in Wales will lead to greater institutional differentiation, still less to a reversion to a tripartite system. In fact, the direction of travel is moving towards much greater collaboration between schools, colleges and private training providers in the delivery of the post-compulsory curriculum (as well as elements of the 14–16 curriculum). Moreover, it is inconceivable in Wales that local authorities will not continue to play a central role in the delivery of education and training (except in higher education). Although the FE colleges remain outside local authority control, the emphasis on collaboration and organisational integration continues and will, no doubt, be a factor in the outcome of the review of FE college governance. Local authorities remain key partners in the development and implementation of all the strategies currently being instigated by the Welsh Assembly Government (WAG).

The development of skills in workplaces is also likely to continue to be a key priority for the WAG. The economic circumstances in which this development takes place, however, are likely to be significantly different from other parts of the UK. Hence, while skills demands from employers will remain a major concern of public policy, the effectiveness of initiatives in this area will continue to reflect the relative poverty of the Welsh economy and the enduring difficulties experienced in generating significant economic growth. It will be interesting in this regard to observe the implementation of the recent Economic Renewal Policy, because it represents a shift in the balance of different types of government interventions to promote economic development in Wales.

More generally too, patterns of economic development – and changes in the financing of the public sector, more specifically – will determine the extent to which the WAG will have the resources to deliver its 'Welsh route' to the development of education and training provision. For this reason, there are likely to be particular 'flashpoints' in the relations between Cardiff and Westminster over the determination of levels of funding through the block grant and the Barnett Formula, both in the run-up to and the aftermath of the election for the National Assembly for Wales to be held in 2011.

In Scotland there is little indication that the policy initiatives the Coalition Government is introducing in England will have any significant impact in the foreseeable future. It has been indicated in Chapters 3 and 5 that the process of policy formation and the institutional structures are, in many respects, quite different from England. This reflects not just divergences since devolution, but a longer history of development. As a result, many of the proposed changes in the schools sector and in the frameworks for governance of post-compulsory education and lifelong learning are really of little relevance in the Scottish context. The ideological thrust of the developments in England also has little support in Scotland.

There is, however, no doubt that the impact of the cuts in public expenditure will have significant implications for the organisation and provision of post-compulsory education and lifelong learning. The Scottish Government has delayed the imposition of financial restrictions, partly with the Scottish Parliamentary elections in May 2011 in mind. It is likely that it will only be after the 2011 elections, when a new government is in place, that clear, new policy initiatives will emerge. While it seems probable that the new government, of whatever political persuasion, will seek to encourage new approaches to delivering provision that will both achieve greater efficiency and help tackle the issue of economic revival and growth, these are likely to involve further evolution within the system rather than radical change. We have already noted the relative strength of the college sector in Scotland, and government policy has been to continue to support this sector insofar as that is possible. We have also noted in earlier chapters the extensive curriculum reform associated with the introduction of the 'Curriculum for Excellence', and this is likely to continue to be a major aspect of policy development in Scotland. It is probable that initiatives around skills development and vocational training will retain major importance and, in this respect, measures may be taken to improve the impact of the services currently provided by Skills Development Scotland. However, in all of these respects the major impact of the policies of the Coalition Government seems likely to be in the reductions in public expenditure and the consequences which these will have on Scotland's post-compulsory and lifelong learning system.

Future scenarios

Several months into the new UK Coalition Government, and following its decision to substantially reduce the public debt over the period of one Parliament, it is possible to view the relationships between the four countries of the UK during successive Labour Governments in a new light.

During a period in which parliamentary devolution was achieved for Scotland, Wales and Northern Ireland, and for most of which there was sustained economic growth (albeit on a fragile basis), the process of divergence between the countries now appears to have been largely about different political emphases. The previous Labour Government's policies have been seen as a mixture of neo-liberal and social democratic ideas, sometimes referred to as the 'Double Shuffle' (Hall, 2003). Meanwhile, Wales and Scotland continued to emphasise the latter over the former and through this to develop a distinctive narrative and approach to education and training policy. Moreover, the relatively buoyant condition of the economy, although affluence was not equally shared between nations and regions, permitted somewhat different interpretations of skill development and varying approaches to curriculum and qualifications, organisation, accountability and governance to emerge.

The election outcome changed all of this. We will suggest, as has already been stated in Chapter 7, that the economic crisis and the UK Coalition Government's approach to public debt reduction could alter the dynamic between the countries of the UK. We outline two possible scenarios for the next five years based on the degree to which the Government's economic strategy succeeds or fails.

Scenario 1: Debt reduction, private sector growth and a successful education and training market

The UK Coalition Government's hope is that the rapid reduction of the public debt, a reduced role for the state, together with incentives to the private and third sectors, will produce a virtuous circle. First and foremost, the UK will retain its high international credit rating, and the reduction in the role of the public sector will provide the space for the private sector to flourish and to move into new areas of activity. The resultant high rates of growth (for example, 3 per cent, or more, annually) will drive down unemployment by the end of the Parliament and increase employer demand for skills. The lifting of the burden of bureaucracy and state planning will allow autonomous institutions and communities, as part of a strong education and training market, to respond in innovative and locally responsive ways. This is seen as part of David Cameron's 'Big Society' agenda (Cameron, 2010). Strengthening learner demand for education and training through Lifelong Learning Accounts will also hold institutions to account, ensuring that poor provision is eradicated and driving up the quality of learning.

Scenario 2: Debt reduction, double-dip recession and a reduced education and training system

An alternative, and far less optimistic, outcome is the prospect of a double-dip recession. In this scenario there is a downward spiral in which an overly rapid reduction in government spending leads to a sharp increase in unemployment, reduces consumer confidence and demand which, in turn, prevents the growth in the private sector needed to fill the gap left by a diminishing state. This scenario not only has an effect at the national level, but also becomes part of a new international economic crisis as a number of economies in the Eurozone follow a similar path.

The impact on education and training would be immediate because employer demand for skills would reduce and there would be fewer jobs and employer-supported Apprenticeship places and less employer training (Mason and Bishop, 2010). On top of this there would be sharp reductions in education and training expenditure, leading to fewer providers and less provision. The state would be unable to respond adequately to the downturn and learners, many of them unemployed, would be unable to gain places on courses in post-compulsory and higher education. In such a context, Lifelong Learning Accounts might become a weak or even worthless currency. Providers would be forced to compete aggressively to remain financially viable, with an emphasis on cost reduction rather than quality or equity. Moreover, the preference of the UK Coalition Government for institutional diversity in England could also result in duplication of provision and the retention of inefficiencies within the system.

Regarding the potential impact of these two scenarios, it could be argued that Scenario 1 would, at best, be realised in parts of England, notably in London and the South East, where the private sector may be sufficiently strong to support it. Aspects of Scenario 2 are more likely in many other parts of the UK because of relatively low levels of private economic activity and the current compensatory role of the public sector (Harris, 2010).

Is there a Scenario 3?

Scenarios 1 and 2 are economically determinist and arguably downplay the state in the respective countries, either at national or local level, taking a more pro-active approach to the labour market, skills policy and education and training provision. The evidence provided in this book, however, suggests that there is a real possibility of a third scenario, in which the processes of divergence in governance and policy produce distinctive responses to the budgetary crisis in Scotland, Wales and Northern Ireland, which differ markedly from that adopted for England by the UK Coalition Government. Here there may be both political and popular support for the devolved governments to use more social democratic strategies. Even in England, there could be different approaches taken at institutional, local and city region levels based on the prevailing values of key policy-makers, institutional managers, trade unions and local government representatives.

With regard to Scotland, Wales and Northern Ireland, policy-makers could decide that, even within greatly reduced budgets, active labour market planning and collaborative policies could be used to mitigate the effects of a weaker private sector and the power of an unregulated market. In all three countries, while the amount of funding for education and training will be less, devolved governments will have a degree of power over the distribution of resources between education and other devolved policy portfolios as well as over how, within education and training, they incentivise providers and determine which areas of policy or groups of learners take priority. For example, the skills utilisation policies currently being pursued in Scotland (and, more modestly, in Wales), the provision of high-quality education and training programmes for the unemployed in Scotland and Wales, the more unified approach to the curriculum and the emphasis on collaboration between providers in all three countries could be continued or even strengthened. In this sense, Scenario 3 could be seen as resulting in a more managed and equitable approach to education and training and labour market policy based on direct intervention, degrees of state planning, a partnership approach and higher levels of political participation. While individual localities and city regions in England may find it more difficult to pursue this approach, because of the strong central steer by the UK Coalition Government and its pursuit of the ideology of the market, echoes of these strategies may also be possible when there is the political will to make them happen.

New directions in learning, skills and lifelong learning: Divergence, convergence and uncertainty

So far we have talked in this book about what could be characterised as a manageable form of divergence between the four countries of the UK. By 'manageable' we are referring to accepted differences in governance, policy and policy-making between England and the other three countries, particularly Wales and Scotland, without these threatening the UK as a political entity. In hindsight, however, we are able to see that these divergences were ameliorated not only by the act of parliamentary devolution itself, but also by the benefits accrued from economic growth and an increase in public expenditure under successive Labour Governments. All of this was to change dramatically in 2010 with the election of a UK Coalition Government and its early announcement of a deficit-reducing budget (Directgov, 2010).

It may be possible to talk about three trends in terms of the directions for learning, skills and lifelong learning policy in the UK. The first refers to the recent experiences under Labour Governments and, in particular, the period since parliamentary devolution in 1999. There are several shared UK features of the respective home systems, particularly when viewed from a continental European perspective, and most notably in regard to the labour market and work-based routes. Nevertheless, during this period differences grew in relation to organisation, governance and also, in the case of Wales, qualifications. These differences were not principal sources of tension, but nor were they sources of policy learning (Raffe and Spours, 2007). They were simply accepted and seen as a legitimate outcome of devolution. In the Scottish case, however, the election of a minority Scottish National Party Government in 2007 changed the tone of policy in that country with more demands for greater powers for the Scottish Government. Chapter 7 emphasises that the UK Labour Government of the time had considerable political interest in managing this relationship, because any fragmentation of the UK could rob it of its Scottish and Welsh strongholds and consign it to opposition for a generation or more in an English government, if general elections became nationally based.

A second trend could be seen to be opening up with the election of the UK Conservative–Liberal Democrat Coalition Government because its early policies on education and lifelong learning will lead to further accumulating differences between England, on the one hand, and Scotland and Wales on the other. The Government in Westminster is about to embark on a wave of market-based reforms (for example, academies and Free Schools), together with qualifications changes (for example, to A Levels) that may deepen the academic/vocational divide. It is hard to imagine Wales and Scotland following suit. Instead, they are likely to hold to the course they have pursued since 1999 which, as we have seen, has already produced significant divergence. The result will be that the education and training systems in those countries begin to look more dramatically different from England's.

A third trend might open up around the economy and public expenditure. As Chapter 7 argues, what could have been regarded as a unifying or integrating factor under Labour Governments could suddenly become a point of major tension between England and the three other countries of the UK, because of the relative importance of public expenditure and investment to the latter. In response, there are already signs that the Scottish Government will push for full fiscal independence and it is difficult not to imagine that Wales too will be looking for a greater acquisition of powers over its economic future, as the Holtham Commission (Independent Commission on Funding and Finance for Wales, 2010) has indicated. What could occur is that more social democratic political formations in Scotland and Wales could employ a radically different political interpretation with regard to the role of the national state, local government, public services and skills, in which different political values and social priorities will be brought to the fore.

Of course, how this unfolds will depend on political developments in all three countries. The relationships might continue to be managed and even some sort of convergence could emerge based on a number of 'ifs': if the UK Coalition Government plans are successfully resisted in England and elsewhere in the UK; if greater fiscal powers are indeed devolved; if the respective government responses to the 'new austerity' have common features; and if the Labour parties in Scotland and Wales recover sufficiently to push back nationalist sentiment. All these 'ifs' are possible, but the balance of probability may be against all of them happening together.

Whatever the outcome, we are undoubtedly entering a much more unstable and uncertain period. It may be overly dramatic to talk about the potential break-up of the UK in its broader sense, but as Chapter 7 points out, the looming radical reduction in public expenditure will put pressure on the UK as a political entity. Greater divergence and, in all likelihood, the devolution of greater powers to Scotland, Wales and Northern Ireland, could also reinforce the realisation that the missing link in the devolution debate is the absence of an entity called 'the English Government'.

However, increasing divergence, which is the most probable outcome, should not deter us from seeking to promote policy learning and collaboration as part of what we have termed 'post-devolution politics'. This is particularly important in relation to post-compulsory education and lifelong learning where there are not only clear UK-wide interests (for example, in relation to skills and the economy), but also strong examples of good practice emerging in each of the four countries that merit wider consideration across the UK. In an era of financial constraint, however this might be mediated in each of the different countries, there are clear advantages in using the knowledge already present within the UK to improve the quality of the education and training systems in each of the four countries. Perhaps it is time that politicians stopped thinking that the grass is always greener elsewhere and paused to reflect on what can be learnt from an examination of policies and practices closer to home.

Note

1   Free Schools are an idea based on the Swedish system: they are independent of local authorities and funded directly from the Department for Education. Sets of parents, community groups or other organisations have been invited to submit plans for such schools to the Secretary of State for consideration. To date, very few groups have come forward.

References

Bassett, D., Cawston, T., Thraves, L. and Truss, E. (2009) *A New Level*. London: Reform.

Bell, D. (2010) 'Devolution in a downturn'. In G. Lodge and K. Schmuecker (eds), *Devolution and Practice 2010*. London: IPPR.

British Broadcasting Corporation (BBC) (2010) 'Northern Ireland spending cuts: Q&A'. <http://www.bbc.co.uk/news/10147838> (accessed 14 September 2010).

Cabinet Office (2010) *The Coalition: Our Programme for Government*. <http://www.cabinetoffice.gov.uk/media/409088/pfg_coalition.pdf> (accessed 8 September 2010).

Cable, V. (2010) 'Speech to Cass Business School', 3 June. <http://nds.coi.gov.uk/content/Detail.aspx?ReleaseID=413641&NewsAreaID=2> (accessed 8 September 2010).

Cameron, D. (2010) 'The Big Society' speech. 19 July. <http://www.number10.gov.uk/news/speeches-and-transcripts/2010/07/big-society-speech-53572> (accessed 5 August 2010).

Chambers, J. (2010) 'Cameron calls for services to become more locally accountable'. David Cameron's speech to Civil Service Live Conference, Olympia, London, 7 July.

Coffield, F., Edward, S., Finlay, I., Hodgson, A., Steer, R. and Spours, K. (2008) *Improving Learning, Skills and Inclusion: The impact of policy*. London: Routledge/Falmer.

Conservative Party (2008) *Building Skills, Transforming Lives: A training and apprenticeship revolution*. Conservative Party Green Paper No. 7. London: Conservative Party.

-- (2010) *The Sir Richard Sykes Review of GCSE and A Levels*. <http://www.conservatives.com/SearchResults.aspx?cx=003491542875545404075%3Ae6gksbreqpy&cof=FORID%3A10&ie=UTF-8&q=Sykes%20Review&sa=Search> (accessed 19 October 2010).

De Waal, A. (2009) *Straight A's? A Level teachers' views on today's A Levels*. London: Civitas.

Department for Education (DfE) (2010a) 'Government announces changes to qualifications and curriculum'. 7 June. <http://www.education.gov.uk/16to19/qualificationsandlearning/a0061424/government-announces-changes-to-qualifications-and-the-curriculum> (accessed 19 October 2010).

-- (2010b) 'Gibb: Further freedoms for schools and colleges'. 24 June. <http://www.education.gov.uk/16to19/qualificationsandlearning/a0061416/gibb-further-freedoms-for-schools-and-colleges> (accessed 19 October 2010).

-- (2010c) 'Michael Gove invites all schools to become academies'. 26 May. <http://www.education.gov.uk/news/news/academies> (accessed 8 September 2010).

Department for Employment and Learning (DEL) (2010) *Success Through Skills 2: The Skills Strategy for Northern Ireland*. Consultation Document. Belfast: DEL.

Directgov (2010) *2010 June Budget Statement*. 22 June. <http://www.direct.gov.uk/prod_consum_dg/groups/dg_digitalassets/@dg/@en/documents/digitalasset/dg_188595.pdf> (accessed 8 September 2010).

Gallagher, C. (2010) 'Curriculum and assessment change processes in Northern Ireland: Will the assessment tail continue to wag the curriculum dog?'. Conference paper presented at the ECER conference, Helsinki, 27 August.

Garner, R. (2010) 'Baker tells Gove he wants to take over failing schools'. *Independent*, 16 June. <http://www.independent.co.uk/news/education/education-news/baker-tells-gove-he-wants-to-take-over-failing-schools-2001611.html> (accessed 8 September 2010).

Gove, M. (2010a) 'Speech to Teach First annual awards at Westminster Academy', 6 September. <http://www.education.gov.uk/news/speeches/mg-westminsteracademy> (accessed 8 September 2010).

-- (2010b) 'Review of vocational education: Letter to Prof. Alison Wolf'. 9 September, <http://www.education.gov.uk/news/news/~/media/Files/lacuna/news/Letter%20to%20AW.ashx> (accessed 14 September 2010).

-- (2010c) 'Letter to Marion Davis, President of the Association of Directors of Children's Services', 19 July. London: DfE.

Graystone, J. (2010) 'Across the Severn, FE is in an enviable state'. *FE Focus, Times Educational Supplement*, 20 August. <http://www.tes.co.uk/article.aspx?storycode=6055199> (accessed 31 August 2010).

Hall, S. (2003) 'New Labour's Double Shuffle', London: LW ebook, Soundings. <http://www.lwbooks.co.uk/journals/articles/nov03.html> (accessed 8 September 2010).

Harris, J. (2010) 'Why the north–south divide will soon become a chasm'. *Guardian*, 9 August. <http://www.guardian.co.uk/commentisfree/2010/aug/08/north-south-divide-soon-become-chasm> (accessed 9 August 2010).

Hayes, J (2010a) 'Speech to City and Islington College'. 17 June. <http://www.berr.gov.uk/news/speeches/john-hayes-city-and-islington-college> (accessed 8 September 2010).

-- (2010b) Letter to FE Sector, 17 June. London: Department for Business, Innovation and Skills.

Independent Commission on Funding and Finance for Wales (2010) 'Fairness and accountability: A new funding settlement for Wales'. <http://wales.gov.uk/icffw/home/report/fundingsettlement/?lang=en> (accessed 19 October 2010).

Leitch, S. (2006) *Prosperity for All in the Global Economy: World class skills*. Final Report. London: The Stationery Office.

Mason, G. and Bishop, K. (2010) *Adult Training, Skills Updating and Recession in the UK: The implications for competitiveness and social inclusion*. Centre for

Learning and Life Chances in Knowledge Economies and Societies, <http://www.llakes.org.uk> (accessed 29 November 2010).

Newsam, P. (2010) 'Learning curve on the Academies Bill 28th July'. Letter to *Guardian*. <http://www.guardian.co.uk/education/2010/jul/28/learning-curve-on-academies-bill> (accessed 8 September 2010).

Raffe, D. and Spours, K. (eds) (2007) *Policy-making and Policy Learning in 14–19 Education*. London: Institute of Education, University of London.

Richmond, T. and Freedman, S. (2009) *Rising Marks and Falling Standards*. London: Policy Exchange.

Scottish Government (2007*) Skills for Scotland*. Edinburgh: The Scottish Government.

Webb Review (2007) *Promise and Performance: The report of the Independent Review of the Mission and Purpose of Further Education in Wales*. Cardiff: WAG.

Willetts, D. (2010) 'University Challenge: Speech at Oxford Brookes University'. 10 June. <http://www.berr.gov.uk/news/speeches/david-willetts-oxford-brookes-university-challenge> (accessed 8 September 2010).